The

Essential

School

Board

Book

The Essential School Board Book

BETTER GOVERNANCE IN THE AGE OF ACCOUNTABILITY

Nancy Walser

HARVARD EDUCATION PRESS

Library of Congress Control Number **2009931670**

Paperback ISBN 978-1-934742-32-7
Library Edition ISBN 978-1-934742-33-4

Published by Harvard Education Press,
an imprint of the Harvard Education Publishing Group

Harvard Education Press
8 Story Street
Cambridge, MA 02138

Cover Design: Perry Lubin

The typefaces used in this book are Sabon and Gill Sans.

For my first teachers:

Ardyce M. Walser
Teacher, Eanes Independent School District, 1977–1988

Rodger M. Walser
Annis and Jack Bowen Professor of Electrical Engineering and Material Science, University of Texas at Austin, 1968–2009

Doris M. Lyon
Teacher, Eaton County, 1928–1932

Theodore H. Lyon
Eaton Rapids, MI, Board of Education, 1950–1956

Top 10 Reasons to Be a School Board Member

10. Because I really like to sit on hard chairs for extended periods of time.

9. Because there are very few foods I don't enjoy, or at least, won't eat.

8. Because I enjoy being at numerous evening events. (You may have a problem if your spouse enjoys you being at these meetings.)

7. Because I like a challenge.

6. Because educators made a real difference in my life.

5. Because I have the gift to listen, hear, and understand positions that are different from my own.

4. Because I have the ability to be ardent in my beliefs or opinions, but also the ability to compromise when necessary.

3. Because I want our children and young people to be successful in school *and* I don't care who gets the credit.

2. Because I realize that every child has the ability and right to as good an education as we can provide.

1. Because I believe I can make a difference in the education of the children and young people where I live.

Source: William J. Phalen, Sr., Calvert County (MD) Board of Education. Used with permission.

Contents

Foreword

Over the course of the last year or so, I have had the privilege of reading and kibitzing on drafts of this book. Nancy Walser comes to this task as a talented writer, editor, former school board member and, incidentally, a student of politics and policy at the Harvard Graduate School of Education, where we managed at least not to destroy her fluent writing style. She deserves ample credit for including me in this process because I am a true skeptic on the subject of local school boards. Most of my work for the last several years has consisted of engaging with teachers and administrators in the hard and often frustrating work of school improvement. In this work, I have seen the full range of relationships between boards and educators, and, in my experience, it is not a pretty picture. Many of the chronic obstacles to continuous, sustained improvement of student learning and performance in schools can be traced to the dysfunctions of local governance structures, including highly factionalized boards, members more interested in building their individual political careers than in learning the complexities of the work, instability in leadership caused in part by the short electoral cycles of school boards in comparison to the longer-term work of school improvement, and seemingly arbitrary shifts in the temperament, focus and purpose of school boards accompanying shifts in board membership. These dysfunctions have had a profound, largely negative impact on the schools I have worked with.

At the same time I have been engaged with American schools, I have also been working on similar issues in the state of Victoria, Australia. One of the distinguishing features of the Victorian model of governance is the complete *absence* of locally-elected school boards, or *any* local governance or administrative structure at all. The sixteen hundred or so public schools of Victoria are governed directly from the state, through a surprisingly lean regional structure, and the resources that would be spent on maintaining local school districts in the U.S. are instead spent on providing services to local schools to support their work in schools and classrooms. Principals exercise a great deal more authority in this structure than they do in the United States, and are generally distinguished by their command of both managerial and instructional expertise. In this system, the state has to earn its authority toward schools by producing value for them. Accountability is truly reciprocal. I have searched for the liabilities of this model in relation to the U.S. model, and I have yet to find them. My Australian experience has reinforced my skepticism about the long-term viability of local school governance nationally. What impresses me about the U.S. system is not how well the local governance structures serve the purposes of adapting broad state and federal policies to local conditions, but how little local boards actually perform this function and how much they tend to focus on the hyper-specialized interests of specific board members and the micropolitics of highly mobilized local constituencies. In most of the American districts in which I work, individual boards members can't describe the superintendent's improvement strategy, much less make a clear account of their role in it.

Against this backdrop, Nancy Walser has done an heroic job of documenting and proposing an alternative future for the American school board, and for the future of local school governance in the States. She has mined the all-too-sparse literature on school boards, and she has spoken directly to practitioners and board members across a broad cross section of communities in all parts of the country. Her tone is deliberate and thoughtful, acknowledging the criticisms that local governance faces, but at the same time making the case that boards can play a more positive role in local school improvement. Hers is a practical, hard-headed approach. She acknowledges the major criticisms of local governance structures and then, point by point, describes local practices that speak directly to these criticisms. Weak and fractious board superintendent relations? Find a system that has worked out an explicit set of norms and protocols for interaction between superintendents and their boards. Micromanaging of operational issues by board members? Find a system that has clearly delineated the boundaries between policy and management. Weak knowledge and expertise about the details of school improvement strategies and practices among board members? Find a system that has trained its board members in the details of the strategy and made regular accounts of the progress of school reform a part of its working agenda. Drifting and meandering board agendas? Build a system of clear goals, benchmarks, and performance measures that boards and administrators can use to focus their work. It turns out to be true, as Walser amply demonstrates, that in a universe of fifteen thousand local school districts one can find solutions to all the major problems that local governance raises. This is both a heartening and a discouraging finding. That these solutions exist, and that they grow out of the hard work and ingenuity of local administrators and board members, is heartening. That they are not common practice is discouraging.

Walser demonstrates through the words of her respondents that there is broad agreement among board members and their various representative bodies at the state and national level that the advent of performance-based accountability in education has dramatically changed the ground rules under which local boards work. Since the early-to-mid 1980s, the states, with the encouragement of the federal government, have more or less completely bypassed local school districts, and their elected boards, in the design and implementation of accountability systems. Virtually every state now has policies that allow it to intervene directly in schools, conducting reviews, imposing remedies and solutions, even closing schools, without so much as a courtesy call at the local board. States, and now the federal government, are deliberately moving significant numbers of public schools out of the local governance structure altogether through various chartering arrangements. In many urban, suburban, and rural areas, demography alone is reducing local school enrollments to the point where the local governance structure seems to be increasingly at risk, and where, more importantly, it is difficult to generate the kinds of economies of scale necessary to build and implement a school improvement strategy. In three of the states in which I work, the smallest school districts have fewer students enrolled systemwide than the *average school* in the largest districts, yet all these districts have the same governance structure with a superintendents and a locally elected board. One wonders how long this situation can endure. The question raised by these changes in policy and demography is not whether local school boards will survive. The federal government and the states have chosen deliberately not to address that question, anticipating the visceral political backlash it is likely to provoke.

No, the question raised by these changes is whether, having survived, local boards will continue to monopolize the delivery of public education. And the answer to that question is clearly no.

The world of educational governance has changed, in historical terms, almost overnight. Local boards will have to learn to operate in a new environment—one in which all types of educational services, including their core business of running schools, are being aggressively privatized, in which traditional jurisdictional boundaries among levels of government no longer hold, allowing one level of government to interfere more or less at will in the affairs of another, and in which many of the services that schools have traditionally provided will begin to migrate into virtual networks where learners can exert much more control over the terms and conditions of their learning than they can in schools.

Nancy Walser makes a persuasive account of the level of ingenuity and inventiveness that some local districts have mustered to respond to these challenges. The practices she documents could form the basis for a reinvention of the role of local school boards in the new environment of public education. I am no less skeptical about local boards, having read Walser's book, but I am a much better informed skeptic, and, perhaps one who is slightly more willing to be persuaded of the future viability of local school governance. That is a major accomplishment. If you are concerned about the future of public education in this country, read this book.

Richard F. Elmore
Gregory R. Anrig Professor of Educational Leadership
at Harvard University
July 2009

Introduction: Why Write a Book About School Boards?

Hundreds of years ago, not too far from where I sit writing this book, early colonists made a rather simple, pragmatic decision that is still controversial in political and education circles today: local schools would be overseen by small groups of local citizens.

Among the first school boards was one organized in 1645 in Dorchester, Massachusetts. Citizens there decided to pick three "able and efficient men" to be "wardens or overseers of the grammar school, according to George Emery Littlefield's account, *Early Schools and School-Books of New England*.[1] The overseers had five duties during their lifetime terms: to find an "able" schoolmaster, keep up the schoolhouse (appealing to the selectmen to tax the townspeople when time came for repairs), order enough wood for the winter, make sure the schoolmaster "faithfully performs his duty," and arbitrate parent complaints. This New England tradition was replicated and evolved across the country.

By the mid-1800s, though, the power to oversee schools had begun to disperse—first to the newly professionalized superintendent (the Progressive Era) and then to the courts (desegregation, Individuals with Disabilities Education Act, or IDEA), state government (standards movement), and the federal government (Title I, No Child Left Behind).

Most notably, reforms of the past two decades have left out a role for approximately 15,000 school boards now operating, as Deborah Land noted in her comprehensive 2002 overview of the history and research about school boards entitled, "Local School Boards Under Review."[2] Empirical research connecting school board practices to increasing student achievement is thin but growing.

The American school board as an institution, however, continues to this day though its public image has taken a beating. Boards are now being held accountable for the performance of their students on annual state tests, with deficiencies routinely publicized and dissected. As they did in the Progressive Era, "elites" and high-profile business leaders argue that schools (and boards) have failed to prepare students to meet the needs of a changing U.S. economy, pointing to the need to impart "twenty-first-century skills" to students so they can compete in a newly "flat" global economy. As an increasing percentage of schools fail to make Adequate Yearly Progress (AYP) as required by the No Child Left Behind Act, and as the number of alternatives like charter schools and virtual schools grow, some of the harshest critics question the relevance of elected boards, in particular.[3] That a few highly dysfunctional boards make front-page news each year doesn't help.

Equally relevant, though, is another question: can school boards, the vast majority of which are elected from and accountable directly to those whose send their children to local public schools and/or support them with their tax dollars, operate effectively in ways that can help raise student achievement in their districts? The answer, and the subject of this book, is yes.

In this book you will read stories of what I call high-functioning (as opposed to dysfunctional or merely functional) school boards whose students are excelling. The sixteen boards featured in this book were drawn from about one hundred recommendations gathered from board association directors, government officials, and other organizations and experts who work with boards. Whether they base student achievement gains on state tests or define them more broadly, these boards are featured in the following pages because they and their districts have been recognized for their improvements: some have won the Broad Prize for Urban Education; some have appeared on state-generated lists of "gap-closing" schools; others are recognized leaders in board development. All together, they represent a fascinating variety of boards in charge of public schools across the United States, both appointed and elected, from rural areas to big cities to sprawling suburbs. (See Appendix E: Districts at a Glance).

Despite their differences, you may be surprised to read in these pages how similar they are. They face different challenges, have different structures, goals, meetings, and rules; yet a remarkable consensus exists among them about policies and practices that help them to focus their efforts—and those of the district and their community—on how their students are doing. Much of what these boards do correlates with practices linked so far by researchers to districts with higher levels of achievement.

Unlike other books about schools boards, this one is meant to be different. Many experts and consultants in the field have written guidebooks that cover the nuts and bolts of being a board member. Some of the ones I've found most helpful are included in Appendix F at the back of this book. I did not feel that another procedural guidebook was necessary.

There have also been some informative and entertaining books written by board members about their personal experiences. Although I did serve on a school board in Cambridge, Massachusetts, for eight years, I did not want to write a book based solely on my own experience. Looking back now, I only wish I had had this book to help me.

What *is* needed, in my opinion, are more concrete examples of successful boards—those boards that is, whose work has contributed appreciably to student improvement. How, exactly, are some boards able to lead their districts in ways that enable more students to achieve at higher levels? What do these boards have in common? Given that most board members essentially volunteer their time and that turnover is inevitable, how do these boards sustain their gains by organizing their work to be efficient and replicable? These were the questions at the top of my mind as I began the research for this book.

The advice in the following pages comes from the experience of local leaders in the trenches. These dedicated public servants, many of them chairs or former chairs of their school boards, have wrestled for years with the challenges of changing policies, procedures, and traditions of local governance to fit the nation's top educational priority of increasing the quality of education for all, not some, students in their districts. The stories in this book are meant to show, rather than tell, how it can be done.

In documenting the commonalities among high-functioning boards, this book also makes a number of arguments. One of the most important is that board structure—whether members are appointed or elected, whether elected from zones or at large—appears to matter less than practices. This is important because so much of the public discourse around school boards focuses on structures rather than practices.[4] Generally speaking, all board structures have well-documented pros and cons.

Members of high-functioning boards tend to recognize the limitations of their particular structure and compensate, understanding that, for example, even those members elected from one part of the community must still keep the interests of all children from the community at the top of their to-do list. One of my favorite quotes from this project comes from a savvy board member who observed, "It's not structure that limits you; it's what you do when you get on." Details of the practices most common to high-functioning boards make up the six chapters. These practices are also highlighted in the three headings that begin chapters 2 through 6.

This book also shows how the role of a school board is changing from that of an "overseer" of the superintendent—a holdover model from nineteenth-century Progressive Era reforms—to that of a coleader with the superintendent. School boards in this book are not aloof, but fully engaged. The accountability movement has made them equally responsible with the superintendent for making sure all students in their district achieve, although the movement, as Land points out, has not included school boards as "potential facilitators of reform." Nevertheless, it's a duty that many take seriously. In order to have a chance of getting to 100 percent proficiency in each district by 2014—the law of the land as it stands now—a school board is dependent on the expert technical knowledge and leadership of its superintendent to make the requisite changes, while the superintendent needs the authority and leadership of the board to make those changes stick. One party can't do it without the support and dedicated efforts of the other.

Although they are coleaders, both the superintendent and the school board still have important and distinct roles that are openly agreed upon and strictly maintained. The most common way of explaining these roles is to divide up the world of schools into the *what* and the *how*. A board is concerned with the what, while the superintendent is in charge of the how. For example, boards are concerned with questions such as what are the primary challenges of the district and what resources can be rounded up to meet them? How challenges are solved in schools and how resources are dispersed are central functions of the school administration and staff, led by the superintendent. Boards recognize that gray areas exist, however. What kinds of information and data and how much a board needs to make decisions and monitor progress is one of the most sensitive of these gray areas. High-functioning boards are able to negotiate with the superintendent ways of operating to the satisfaction of both parties.

Finally, as one board member in this book expresses so eloquently—school boards have untapped power. They have been overlooked as partners in reform, and yet, when they are involved constructively and appropriately in focusing the attention of the district on student achievement, great things happen. In this respect, more school reform organizations should find ways of including board members, as the Panasonic Foundation has routinely done. Board service requires hard work and dedication, a willingness to learn, and many long nights of problem solving with lots of people. On the other hand, there are many things boards can do to make service much more manageable—an important consideration given that most board members typically receive little to no pay and have multiple responsibilities, like full-time jobs and family.

The school boards profiled in this book stand as important examples at a critical time in education. And they are only a small slice of those that are working productively. Educators, administrators, policymakers, parents, and interested citizens should be aware that there is a way to put local politics ("with a little *p*," to quote one member) to work for students. School board members in particular need to know and should know about these practices. They need to know that what they do—and what they don't—can limit the success of their students. Others, especially in their own communities, need to remind them. I have written this book to help. And since I know how busy school board members can be, I have tried to keep it short and easy to read.

CHAPTER ONE

Board Practices That Make a Difference for Children

What can a group of noneducators who meet once or twice a month in an office building do to help children in a classroom read better? A lot, it turns out.

Take the case of an army recruit, to borrow an analogy from the authors of the Lighthouse Project, a landmark study begun in 1998 to examine board behavior and student achievement. Chances are a drill sergeant is going to have a greater affect on that recruit's development as a soldier than someone sitting in an office in Washington, D.C. Unless, of course, war is declared, or the army is given a new mission or is dramatically downsized. In other words, there are circumstances when a "distal" player can have a dramatic effect.

The Lighthouse study stands as one of two important efforts by researchers to systematically examine whether and how school boards, "distal" as they may be from classrooms, influence student achievement, according to Deborah Land's 2002 review.[1]

Researchers with the Lighthouse Project of the Iowa Association of School Boards (IASB) began by looking at attitudes and practices in 3 districts with a 3-year record of low achievement, and comparing them to those found in an equal number of similar districts with much higher achievement records. Researchers chose school districts in the state of Georgia to study because it had a reliable database of results on standardized achievement tests administered across the state. The IASB team conducted 159 interviews with board members, superintendents, district staffers, and community members in all 6 districts. Then they gave the responses to researchers to analyze without telling them which districts were the high scorers. To their surprise, the study revealed notable differences between what they called "moving" boards and those that were "stuck."[2]

The IASB team then categorized the beliefs and practices common to moving districts. Boards in these high-achieving districts (as well as their administrators) displayed "elevating" views of students, expressing their belief, for example, that all kids were capable of learning at high levels. Board members also showed they were knowledgeable about seven conditions for school change, synthesized from prior research (see figure 1.1).

FIGURE 1.1 *Seven conditions for school renewal central to achievement*

In 2000, the Lighthouse Project identified "moving" and "stuck" school boards based on evidence that they understood these conditions. In districts where boards were stuck, students had lower achievement as measured by a standardized test.

1. Shared leadership	A focus on student learning through a shared clear vision, high expectations, and dynamic leadership among all levels.
2. Continuous improvement	A continuous focus on improving education, with high levels of involved and shared decision making.
3. Ability to create and sustain initiatives	An understanding of how to organize the people and the school environment to start and sustain an improvement effort.
4. Supportive workplace for staff	A supportive workplace that enables all staff to succeed in their roles.
5. Staff development	Regular schoolwide staff development that is focused on studying teaching and learning.
6. Support for school sites through data and information	Using data and information on student needs to make decisions and modify actions at the district and building level.
7. Community involvement	A close connection between the school, parents, and community.

Source: "IASB's Lighthouse Study: School Boards and Student Achievement," *Iowa School Board COMPASS: A Guide for Those Who Lead* 5, no. 2 (Fall 2000).

IDENTIFYING BOARDS ON THE MOVE

In essence, boards of high-achieving districts in the Lighthouse Project showed they understood important factors in school improvement efforts, as well as their role in those efforts, and could also connect improvement goals to specific efforts going on in classrooms.

Members of moving boards, for example, could mention specific initiatives being implemented in the district and ways that they had contributed to them. They could describe specific goals related to learning, and structures that were in place for improving teaching and learning and communications within the district. They also expressed a desire to improve. Poverty, lack of parent involvement, and other barriers were seen as factors to be overcome rather than excuses for why some students were not achieving at similar levels. They expressed confidence in staff and support for training, and could make links between training and goals for student learning. They used data in decision making and could name specific ways the board and district were attempting to connect with stakeholders in the community.

Members of "stuck boards," on the other hand, exhibited very different behaviors and beliefs. Board members did not know how goals or improvement plans were being implemented, did not believe it was their job to know about instruction, and did not believe it was possible to "reach all kids." They were unaware of how goals and initiatives were being carried out, and only discussed information presented to them by the superintendent. They commented negatively about staff or expressed the opinion that new staff, families, or students would be needed to raise achievement. They had a low regard for staff development and rarely used data to make decisions. Board members were frustrated with the lack of community involvement but had no plans to improve it.

Members of both types of boards expressed the desire to meet the needs of children and were satisfied with their superintendents. Achievement gaps among subgroups were present in both moving and stuck districts. Significantly, attitudes of staff mimicked those of board members.

In phase 2 of the Lighthouse Project, researchers set out to see if student achievement would increase as a result of the facilitators working with boards to instill the beliefs and practices of moving districts. Five pilot districts for the training were identified, with enrollments ranging from four hundred students to thirty thousand.

Facilitators synthesized important research connected to student achievement in order to discuss key issues with board members, such as why teaching is an important component to learning and what factors make up good professional development.

In turn, researchers learned from board members about the kind of help they needed in critical areas such as how to examine data, and what it took to change beliefs about how children learn. In one district, for example, researchers videotaped fourth- and eighth-grade students who were struggling to read required textbooks. "The idea was to get them to feel the pain of the child," said Mary Delagardelle, who served as the original Lighthouse Project director and is now the executive director of the Iowa School Boards Foundation, the research arm of the IASB.

The technique worked. "The high school principal was so taken aback," recalled Delagardelle. "One eighth grader was someone that he didn't recognize as struggling. The principal came back with a textbook and said, 'Here's a sample of what this child will have to read in ninth grade.' We asked the board, 'If something doesn't change for this child, what's going to happen next year?' The board said, 'We're not going to let this happen anymore.' They created a safety net program for older struggling readers. We learned that you have to chip at their beliefs to get them to do something different."

Researchers used four main tools to monitor change in the pilot districts: a districtwide survey related to the seven conditions for school change, a second survey about beliefs and expectations for student learning, direct observation of the boards, and, to gauge the impact of changing beliefs, the annual student achievement data for the district. Progress was slowed by the loss of funding in the third year. One pilot district, the largest in the study, dropped out. Yet researchers were able to document significant changes in practices and beliefs of the remaining pilot districts, especially in the use of data and changed attitudes toward professional development. The pilots also posted significant gains in student achievement above the average for their state, according to Delagardelle, who presented the results at the 2008 National School

Boards Association (NSBA) conference. Even though many variables were at play in the pilot districts at the time, the changes were significant enough to show that they were not coincidental, she said.

In addition, staff members and board members alike showed an increased ability to explain the district's improvement goals. Board members spent more time discussing student achievement with each other in regular board meetings and work sessions. All groups surveyed agreed strongly that local school boards could play a role in increasing achievement.

In 2006, researchers expanded the Lighthouse training into seven states for phase 3 of the project. Personnel from state board associations are being trained to train boards in their states using eleven modules developed from phase 2. Researchers will study the results and compare those found in phase 2 pilot districts. Delagardelle says the Lighthouse Project is still "very much" a research project in need of support. "We've had difficulty getting funding because boards are considered irrelevant even though systemic reforms stress the importance of including stakeholders at all levels," she said.

In the summer of 2009, the IASB was slated to help conduct a first-ever national survey of school board practices in partnership with NSBA, the Fordham Institute, and the Wallace Foundation. Among other things, the survey will explore operational differences between boards, as well as beliefs, priorities, and actions related to improving student achievement.

BOARD PRACTICES IN "WELL-GOVERNED" DISTRICTS

Another significant study of school board practices was published in 1997 by the New England School Development Council (NESDEC) and the Educational Research Service (ERS), according to the Land review. Recommendations from this study were issued in 2000. This group conducted 132 interviews across 5 states in 10 different districts with high and low levels of student achievement as measured by dropout rates, the percentage of students taking college entrance tests, and the percentage of graduates attending 2- or 4-year colleges.

The resulting report identified six characteristics of "well-governed" districts associated with higher student achievement.[3] High-quality boards stood out for their (1) stability (members served at least six to eight years) and desire to serve students rather than seek higher office; (2) short regular meetings coupled with annual or biannual goal-setting retreats; (3) effective management that resulted in referring complaints to the administration, lack of separate subcommittees, and joint discussion of problems with the superintendent as a "governance team"; (4) a communicative board chair who functioned as a critical go-between for the superintendent and his or her colleagues; (5) focus on student achievement as evidenced by policy, the budget, facilities, and support for the superintendent as the district's CEO/educational leader; and (6) an ability to work collaboratively, resulting in a "high degree" of trust.

Board behavior in the low-achieving districts apparently wasn't hard to miss. These boards were "riddled with conflict," engaged in "bickering" and "nit-picking" and allowed their operations to be "overshadowed by personal interests," the authors wrote. "Over and over board members complained that they were not spending their time on what they thought should be their priorities . . . Such micromanagement—usually by one or two members of the board—was criticized by both board members and superintendents as their most common cause of frustration."

RESULTS FROM THE PANASONIC FOUNDATION

A third important effort to document effective board practices based on research has come out of the work of the New Jersey–based Panasonic Foundation, which has twenty-five years' experience consulting with school districts on systemic, sustainable reform. The foundation is small, with an endowment of $20 million given by the North American subsidiary of the Panasonic Corporation of Japan "in a gesture of thanks to the United States and as a way of contributing to the American society."[4] Interestingly, it is one of the few foundations to insist on including the local school board in any district that seeks its help.

Using independent consultants, the foundation establishes long-term partnerships with a small number of urban districts with more than seven thousand students to "create new systems of equity and quality in which all students are educated to high levels—in every school, in every classroom, and regardless of background."[5] Using a protocol and "investigative questions," facilitators work with district leaders in seminars, consultations, and workshops to assess their progress toward fulfilling essential responsibilities that include establishing core values; a culture and climate of "care, commitment, and continuous improvement"; rigorous learning standards and expectations; a shared accountability system and monitoring systems; requisite professional learning; adequate fiscal and other resources; and important partnerships at local, state, and national levels. As a precondition to work with the foundation, the board, the superintendent, central administration, and the union leadership of a district must all commit to being involved. Teachers, parents, and other community partners are also involved. "Our definition is to see school systems as having interdependent leaders and processes necessary to advance student learning," explains Scott Thompson, the foundation's assistant executive director. "When you don't have those systems working together, they aren't sustainable."

The foundation's findings on effective boards are contained in a 2009 draft entitled "Doing the Right Thing: The Panasonic Foundation's Guide for Effective School Boards," and come from the "school of hard knocks," in working with dozens of districts, according to the report.[6] However, their conclusions are in line with the findings of previous empirical studies: effective boards have members that work together to establish a vision and a set of values, to articulate results, and to create the conditions for achieving these results through policy, effective use of resources, community engagement, collaborative relations with the superintendent, and union negotiations. (See figure 1.2.)

"We have worked in districts where schools' improvements were slowed, even stopped by the spin-off effects of board conflict and misbehavior," the authors write. "We have also seen school boards commit to improving student achievement, use all their 'tools' effectively and turn around years of low-performance among schools."

Clearly, there is a growing body of knowledge about how school boards can function best to increase student achievement. Many of the findings are similar.

As you will read, members of high-functioning boards today are well aware of the difference between "bad" and "good" board behavior. They

FIGURE 1.2   *Four sacred duties of a school board*

Duty 1

Establish and promulgate ownership of the district's vision and values.

Duty 2

Articulate expected district results and monitor progress.

Duty 3

Create the conditions for achievement of the district's vision, values, and expected results through effective use of the five areas of board authority—"board tools":

- Promulgation of policies.
- Governing the use of community fiscal resources for education.
- Engaging the community in its schools.
- Sustaining an effective board–executive relationship.
- Negotiating and approving union contracts.

Duty 4

Ensure a community-wide climate of commitment, respect, and trust.

Source: Patricia Mitchell, Andrew Gelber, Sophie Sa, and Scott Thompson, "Doing the Right Thing: The Panasonic Foundation's Guide for Effective School Boards" (draft, the Panasonic Foundation, Secaucus, NJ, 2009).

are familiar with the research on effective board practices and use this knowledge. They believe that what they can do can make a big difference to the current and future students of their community. Whether appointed or elected, they believe their constituents will support them in "doing the right thing" to advocate for the education of every student, but especially for those who need extra support to learn at high levels.

As humans, they aren't perfect. Many have learned the hard way, through times of dysfunction, about what kinds of structures and policies can help them stay on track as a board. They are also well aware of the need to find ways to institutionalize what is working well and sustain momentum toward goals in the face of inevitable changes in district leadership.

In the following chapters, you'll hear their stories and read in detail what they are doing.

CHAPTER TWO

Building a Foundation for Student Success

Collaborating   Conversing   Committing

CALVERT COUNTY, MD • MONTGOMERY, AL • SIMSBURY, CT •
SPRINGDALE, AR • MADISON COUNTY, KY • LAURENS COUNTY
DISTRICT 55, SC

Getting on a school board usually means running for office. As you are campaigning, people will ask what you want to get done. In other words, why should they vote for you? Or you are appointed to a board because you have certain talents or expertise or connections. However you get there, suddenly you are making decisions with four, or six, or eight other people. Suddenly, it's not just about you.

Although individuals who make up school boards may be viewed as influential or powerful by some or many in their own communities, their authority as a board member comes from decisions made as a group, and recorded as votes in a legally posted meeting. It can be a difficult adjustment to make, and a hard fact to remember.

In 1995, researchers from the National School Boards Association (NSBA) surveyed experienced school board members to see what they thought was the hardest thing about learning to be part of a board. Some of the most common responses included "learning to acknowledge publicly that you have no power and authority as an individual board member," "determining what your function is on the board and how to accomplish it effectively," and "that you can't solve everyone's problems by yourself."

Board collaboration with the superintendent may be the hardest thing to achieve; and yet it could very well determine the quality of student learning in your district. In the 1997 NESDEC study comparing districts with high-quality and low-quality governance, trust and collaboration were singled out "above all else" as the most important distinguishing factors of well-governed districts.[1]

One author of that report, Richard Goodman, a longtime superintendent and governance consultant, recently decided to explore what it was like to be on a school board, "the one job in public education I have never experienced," he wrote in a 2007 issue of the *School Administrator.*[2] Serving on the Winnacunnet school board in Hampton, New Hampshire, Goodman said he gained an "emotional understanding" of the job. It was difficult to argue "passionately" for a cause and still end up on the minority side, he wrote. But because of his research experience and work in the field, he knew the importance of maintaining a collaborative working relationship on the board. "Our board had established a sense of trust, commitment and support, and my colleagues knew I would uphold the board decision without reservation."

Collaboration doesn't necessarily mean that everyone agrees all the time. It is easier and less stressful for everyone, of course, but it isn't necessary. Savvy board chairs, for example, anticipate and plan for conflict; some even believe that a certain level of "healthy" conflict helps generate ideas that eventually lead to better policies and budgets. At the end of the day, though, when the camera is on and votes are being cast, it's important for collaboration's sake to come together on a decision. If that isn't possible, high-functioning boards and their superintendents will postpone votes until more information or alternative solutions are found to bring them closer together. Later, in chapter 4, I will write about policies and procedures that high-functioning boards use to help them come together and focus on their important role of collaborating for increased achievement, including norms and values, operating protocols, meeting rules, and goal-setting retreats. These policies and practices are also sometimes necessary for sidestepping diversions that take boards off task, including personal agendas and single issues championed by individual members or by "outliers" determined to throw a wrench into everything.

FROM OVERSEERS TO LEADERS: A NEW ROLE FOR SCHOOL BOARDS

You might ask at this point, What *is* so magical about collaboration? Isn't this a free country? Aren't people elected to speak their minds? The answers are yes, and not necessarily.

Since the passage of the No Child Left Behind (NCLB) Act in 2001, the landscape of education has changed forever in this country. Public school districts—and by extension, their school boards—are now being held accountable for the performance of all students on state tests. Although the standards of proficiency vary state by state, the mandate of NCLB—that all schools must educate all students to high levels—is unprecedented in the history of U.S. education, Richard Elmore and colleagues pointed out.[3] As a result, educators are now being required to do things that they have never done before, says Elmore, who has studied district reforms and, more recently, pioneered the application of "medical rounds" to improve classroom instruction in schools. Data and feedback from superintendents involved in "instructional rounds" networks in several states show that as schools improve over time, the work actually becomes harder, increasing the need for collaborative problem solving by those closest to students, according to Elmore.[4] A primary role of policy makers, then, is to create the *conditions* necessary for this critical work to take place, he argues.[5]

The age of accountability has changed the role of the school board from "overseer who makes sure the rascals don't steal the money" to that of a coleader with the superintendent in charge of raising achievement, according to Joe Villani, deputy executive director of the National School Boards Association and coauthor of NSBA's *The Key Work of School Boards*. The overseer model for school boards emerged during the Progressive Era, when business and university "elites" lobbied to "take schools out of politics" of ward bosses and locals.[6] This period of history, vividly portrayed in David Tyack's classic work, *The One Best System*, extended from 1890 to 1920. During this period, reformers were largely successful in consolidating and remaking school boards in the image of corporate boards, which had one employee, the CEO (or the superintendent of schools), who was held primarily responsible for the success, or failure, of the organization.

Boards are now expected to do more than make policy, sit back, and oversee the superintendent, Villani argues. "The role of the school board member today has to be one of leadership working in tandem with the superintendent to make sure that the public's interests are served by the public schools. They do that by engaging and linking to the community. The board's role is not to box in the superintendent, but work with him or her and find the right solutions, ask the right questions, and focus on the right issues. The board needs to constantly push the system and ask the questions. It's governance, not management."

In the updated 2009 version of NSBA's *Key Work*, Villani and his co-authors urge school board members to take a big-picture "systems" view of a school district and form a leadership team with the superintendent to concentrate on eight areas: vision, standards, assessment, accountability, alignment, climate and culture, community engagement, and continuous improvement. In each area, the authors delineate overlapping but different roles for school boards and their superintendents. (See figure 2.1.) They, too, frame the main responsibility of a modern school board as "creating the conditions within their school districts that enable students to meet rigorous knowledge and performance standards," noting that "it is no longer possible or credible for boards of education to serve as passive reviewers and judges of the work of others."[7]

Interviews with members of high-functioning boards reveal that they are highly attuned to the need to create the conditions for collaboration focused on students. They see it as part of their duty to model collaboration from the top. They are also willing to delegate decision making over more traditional, but less important matters, like which sports team will get new uniforms, in order to free up time on their meeting agendas to focus on student achievement and to send a message that priorities have shifted.

Collaboration isn't always easy, but it's worth it, say these members. They describe an active practice of give and take (or winning and

FIGURE 2.1   *Roles of the board and the superintendent in continuous improvement*

The school board	The superintendent
1. Follows a regular process to review student achievement data to ensure continuous improvement.	a. Recommends to the board a process for continuous improvement.
	b. Sets and reviews benchmarks and performance indicators that demonstrate student progress related to the district's strategic plan and standards.
	c. Provides clear analysis of relevant data related to student achievement.
	d. Seeks input from professional staff on changes needed to strengthen instructional programs.
	e. Recommends changes to instructional program indicated by data and staff input.
2. Takes part in training on principles of continuous improvement including use of data and customer focus.	a. Schedules training on principles of continuous improvement and participates with the board.
	b. Assures ongoing training for all employees on principles of continuous improvement.
	c. Assures professional development to build understanding of information provided by data and to encourage staff participation in needed changes.
3. Participates in work sessions to better understand needed changes in curriculum and instruction based on related data.	a. Presents information to the board on needed curriculum/instruction changes.
	b. Explains data to support recommended changes.
4. Provides funding for continuous improvement.	a. Reviews curriculum and instruction plans and costs as part of the board's budget planning.
	b. Presents budget recommendations to the board on resources needed for continuous improvement.
5. Adopts board policies that support continuous improvement.	a. Recommends policies needed to support continuous improvement efforts.
	b. Conducts periodic review with the board to identify additional policies needed or to revise existing ones.
6. Supports publicly and communicates the value of continuous improvement to the community.	a. Communicates the process and results of the district's continuous improvement efforts to key stakeholders as part of the district's communications plan.
	b. Communicates both proposed and approved curriculum and instruction changes to stakeholders affected, such as students, staff, and parents.

losing) that goes beyond simple information sharing in order to build consensus and move forward on important initiatives. Such effort is rewarded: members of high-functioning boards consistently point to collaboration—with their colleagues and their superintendent—as one of the major factors in their success in raising student achievement. Furthermore, achieving collaboration is seen as *an accomplishment in and of itself.* They tend to speak of their boards' lack of egos or personal agendas in ways that make it sound as if they have reached a final stage of enlightenment.

GETTING TO FIVE (OR SEVEN, OR NINE)

Just listen to Frank Parish describe the way his five-member board operates in Calvert County, Maryland. At the age of eighty, Parish was about to retire as a member and the president of the board at the end of 2008, when I interviewed him. "We have a very unusual board," he told me. "We are recognized in the state as being unique. We are five people without any personal agendas. I can't remember a time when a person's agenda surfaced. Everything in the school system is focused on student achievement. That's our mantra."

Parish, a former air force pilot and MIS professional, appreciated the variety of talents and interests his colleagues bring to the board, which included a former U.S. Census Bureau employee, a medical technician, a lawyer, and a former superintendent. "Each one of us brings to the table the ability to connect the dots in a different way . . . We have hotly discussed issues that have come to us, and we get very excited about these issues, but the thing about it is, it's never personal."

He gave the lion's share of the credit, though, to superintendent Jack Smith. In formal and informal ways, Smith keeps his board "very, very tightly informed of everything that's going on," said Parish. In what he calls a "master stroke for focusing everyone's attention on student achievement," Smith recommended, and the board approved, the use of a database management system that allows teachers to gauge student progress on a regular basis. Teachers share results with each other and use them to target support from learning specialists. Smith is also "very aggressive" at evaluating personnel and "making sure the right people are sitting on the right seat on the bus," said Parish. "When I think of Jack, I think of one thing: leadership. He doesn't manage his people, he leads and supports his people and is extremely organized." With Smith's leadership, the board kept the focus on teaching and learning despite weathering five redistricting plans sparked by growing enrollments since 1999. "Everything in the school system is focused on student achievement; that's our mantra," said Parish.

Smith agreed with Parish's assessment. Despite the need to change school boundaries five times over a ten-year period—an often highly politicized process that can fracture boards and that resulted in a court challenge from parents—the board has remained single-minded in its focus on overall student achievement, Smith said. In particular, the board was instrumental in supporting key initiatives like maintaining the twenty-student limit in first- and second-grade classrooms; creating learning specialist positions to replicate best practices among middle schools; and instituting "core leader" positions at the high school level to support struggling students. "The board has come to understand the language of student achievement; they consistently ask to be shown the data, and we talk about it," said Smith.

As a result, Calvert County students have made tremendous progress during the past five years, said Smith. In 2005, fewer than 50 percent of high schoolers passed the state test; in 2008, that number had increased to 94 percent. The number of students taking advanced placement courses has doubled in the last five years. Schools have consistently made their Adequate Yearly Progress (AYP) targets, and the district now typically tops the charts for every grade level among the twenty-four districts in Maryland.

Other board practices have helped move the district forward, said Smith. The board operates as a whole, with no separate subcommittees, and is good about "practicing the fact that 'you're five; you are never one,'" he said. For example, one board member has a passion for the arts. "When something about the arts comes up, he loses all reason," said Smith, "but then, when it's apparent that the interest is not shared by a majority of three members, he'll say, 'I can count to three'—they actually say that," said Smith. With help from the staff, the board updated all its policies, including a "policy on policies," and put them online.

And, as Parish describes, the glue that helps holds a board of individuals together is also the educational leader of the district, the person in charge of recommending improvement initiatives and explaining them to the board—the superintendent.

WANTED: A COLLABORATIVE SUPERINTENDENT

In Montgomery, Alabama, racial tension and stagnation were major hallmarks of the district until the board hired John Dilworth as superintendent in 2007, according to board president Mary Briers. The previous superintendent's style was "my way or the highway," Briers said. Dilworth, who came to the district via the Broad Superintendents Academy, was different. His arrival ushered in a new period of collaboration that changed everything.

"I've seen the difference because I'm a retired educator," said Briers, who taught for twenty-five years in the district. "Our success is because of our new superintendent. He's been the best. He's willing to listen. He'll bring in his ideas, but if you show yours is better, he'll listen. And if members have a problem [with a proposal], he might withdraw it. We also talk about what's not working, and modify the plans together."

With Dilworth, the Montgomery board crafted a strategic plan with specific outcomes. "The superintendent and his central office staff brought in some ideas that they had for the plan," Briers said as she described the process, "and we added to those things that we thought were important. And then they brought it back to us. It was a team effort." For the plan, Dilworth proposed partnering with the area's businesses community to open career academies at the high school level, as well as a night school for students who needed to catch up with credits for graduation, according to Briers. For its part, the board was looking for more accountability. Schools that had failed to make AYP on state tests were required to present improvement plans with monthly progress reports for the board; "So it was not just like, 'We failed . . . maybe next year,'" said Briers. "We have had strategic plans before, but they didn't have a timeline whereby, at a certain date, we could review it to see if we were close to our mark, or at our mark. There is more accountability with this one, and there was more of a buy-in process with principals and administrators."

Dilworth also made suggestions for board operations to facilitate collaboration and transparency, Briers said. A Committee of the Whole meeting was added to the monthly schedule so that new initiatives could be discussed with the whole board in a nonvoting meeting, rather than in subcommittees with only two members attending. "We all hear everything at the same time, and the administration is open to answering our concerns," Briers explained. "Everybody gets a clear picture of what was going on. Sometimes when you hear the rationale for something, it's easier to get on board versus just reading about something in a subcommittee report," she explained. Regular meetings became shorter because initiatives had already been vetted.

In two short years, Montgomery reading scores have improved tremendously, she said, and the district is also beginning to tackle the thorny issue of lack of seats in magnet schools by addressing how to make teaching as rigorous in the "traditional" schools as in the magnets. Although she's not yet satisfied, she said, "I see progress. We have a ways to go, but there's a team effort because the superintendent is working with his board. He's the best thing that could have happened to us."

In 2009, when I checked back with Briers, she had disappointing news. As sometimes happens, Dilworth had been recruited away by a district in his home state of Louisiana. His family wanted to return, and it was an offer he couldn't refuse, even after the local business community offered him $150,000 to stay and finish the remaining three years of his contract.

Thanks to two years of productive collaboration, however, the district is well positioned to continue making progress, said Briers. Two cabinet members hired by Dilworth will provide stability, and the board is committed to continuing to implement the five-year strategic plan with the next superintendent, she said. "We don't need to reinvent the wheel. We don't want to start over. We have a vision right now, we have great collaboration and camaraderie with our business community, and we want to forge ahead with our blueprint at this point."

Finding and keeping effective superintendents poses a critical challenge for school boards, both elected and appointed. It's not the only ingredient needed to make headway on student achievement, but it's a necessary condition.[8]

Often, in interviews with board chairs, I began by asking a simple, open-ended question: in what ways do you believe your board has contributed to increased student achievement in your district? Jack Sennott, chair of the Simsbury, Connecticut, board, summed up the typical answer best: "First and foremost, your highest responsibility is to hire an excellent chief executive," he said, without skipping a beat. If things go well, the next challenge—as Montgomery found—is keeping them around. Among its many findings, the 1997 NESDEC study found that in well-governed districts, superintendents had served at least ten years.

Then again, life happens. Boards change, superintendents get recruited away. Strategic plans and other practices can help sustain the work of productive boards (more about that in chapter 6), but taking care to find the right superintendent is fundamental.

In its "Guide for Effective School Boards," the Panasonic Foundation urges boards to spend time constructing a clear vision as a "compass" for the district and as a foundation for any productive relationship with a superintendent. It takes two to tango, but a clear, compelling vision— "not hollow platitudes that often get passed off as vision statements"— is the responsibility of the board no matter who is superintendent, the report states. "The Panasonic Foundation has found that the best context for real school improvement occurs when the school board and superintendent are attracted to each other because both are unwavering in their vision of a better district and are conscious that they are mutually dependent for making that vision a reality," the report states.[9]

INVEST IN A SUPER SEARCH

In 2004, Simsbury lost its longtime superintendent. The district was at a critical juncture, Sennott recalls. "We had a twenty-year superintendent. The guy was a legend. Statistically, when you lose someone like that, the next one you get, that's the transitional superintendent. If you stayed twenty years, everybody in the building has been hired by you— they only know how to do things your way. The transitional superintendent gets frustrated and leaves after a few years."

The nice ending to Sennott's story was that the transitional superintendent scenario did not happen. "We interviewed superintendents much more thoroughly than I've seen in business, and we picked the right person." Superintendent Diane Ullman has been leading the district for five years. "She's been unbelievably successful in crafting a real strong administrative group," said Sennott. The superintendent is open to feedback and encourages it from board members, he said. There are very few split votes, he added.

For districts in transition, the key to finding an educational leader who can work comfortably and collaboratively with the school board is executing a thorough search, agrees Eliza Holcomb. Holcomb, who was a private sector recruiter and human resources executive for twenty-two years, now recruits superintendents for school boards through her affiliation with the Connecticut Association of Boards of Education (CABE). CABE is one of more than thirty state school board associations that provide superintendent search services for school boards.

Her job isn't easy. Holcomb finds that the typical pool of candidates numbers between twelve and thirty, down slightly from when she first started working with school boards in 2002. Since the advent of No Child Left Behind, school boards are paying more attention to the skills and abilities of a superintendent to move student achievement. "I've seen a shift with NCLB; there's more discussion about student performance and instructional leadership," said Holcomb. "It's not the volume of candidates, though, it's the quality, and quality comes from a number of variables, such as measurable success in their former positions, their core values, their leadership style, and their ability to collaborate, set vision, and achieve outcomes." Ninety percent of superintendents who she's found for Connecticut boards are still leading the same districts.

To undertake a thorough search, Holcomb starts with a long planning meeting with the board. She begins by asking the group what vision and timeline they have for a search process and how the community will be involved, and tries to get everyone on the same page. Then she meets individually with each board member for an hour to get answers to three questions: What are the strengths of the district, and what do you value the most? What are the issues and challenges? What are you looking for in a superintendent?

These board interviews are followed by targeted focus groups with central office administrators, principals, support staff, teachers, high schoolers, and parents to get their feedback. She meets privately with elected officials and helps organize public forums for anyone in the community to come out and talk about their desires for a new educational leader. All the feedback is put into a spreadsheet to identify common themes. Holcomb then writes a "leadership profile" that summarizes what the district is looking for in its next superintendent.

The leadership profile is a critical tool for helping Holcomb identify the right mix of experiences and the "cultural fit" between superintendent candidates and the district in search of a new leader. "Someone may have all of the experience, knowledge base, and passion, but the style in which they lead may be in great conflict with the culture in the community," said Holcomb. "I've seen really bright people fail because of that. There's an intellectual piece and intuition piece of the process." When she does identify potential candidates for a particular district, Holcomb spends time with each individual discussing the "strengths, opportunities, and challenges" about a district. Holcomb works with school board members to use the profile to craft questions for interviewing finalists. (See box 2.1.)

While the interviews are important, they are only a first step. Holcomb said it's the amount of homework the board does afterward that can really make a difference. After the finalists are selected by the board and their names are made public, it's time for board members to really knuckle down and do their homework. Using the Internet and their own resources, board members should go well beyond the list of individuals that the candidates give as references. "Talk to the full board of the district they are in and other boards they've worked for. Contact the building leadership, union leadership, community and parent leadership," said Holcomb. She also recommends that board members visit the districts that the candidates are currently working in. "Site visits should be coordinated with the people the board wants to meet, not who the candidate wants you to meet," she said. "You really have to witness in a tangible way to see if they've really accomplished what they have said they've accomplished. Site visits can ease concerns or validate them." And while the Internet can provide useful information, it's important for board members to balance what they read with what they hear from other sources—are you getting information from just one disgruntled person posting to the Internet? Data on the Internet about test results

BOX 2.1

Questions for Finding an Achievement-Oriented Superintendent

Here are some questions that were generated by school boards in Connecticut working with superintendent search consultant Eliza Holcomb.

- As a result of increasingly challenging NCLB and [state] benchmarks, what have you done to upgrade the educational programs in schools currently under your supervision? How have you evaluated the results?

- Briefly describe how you would go about developing a comprehensive strategic plan for the district and how you would implement it. Which stakeholders would you involve in the process? Follow-up: how would you monitor and evaluate the implementation of short- and long-range district goals?

- Discuss how you would ensure the relevance of a district's educational program for students in the twenty-first century.

- What creative approaches have you utilized that resulted in increased student achievement and academic success for students?

- How do you know an outstanding teacher/administrator when you see one? What successful strategies have you used to recruit high-quality educators? Follow-up: what do you think the most important factors are in teacher and administrator retention?

- Please describe your management/leadership style. What do you see as your strengths? Weaknesses?

- What do you believe is the role of a highly effective school board?

- Describe how you would obtain support from the school board for important initiatives.

- How do you engage faculty and staff in the organizational decision-making process?

- What steps can the superintendent take to ensure that members of the school board maintain focus on common goals that transcend political agendas?

- What should be the essential components of the annual board and superintendent performance evaluations? How do you feel these evaluations should be carried out?

- Making unpopular decisions comes with the territory. Please give us an example of one you've made and how you handled the fallout.

also has to be weighed, she said, adding, "It's not only one person who creates outcomes in a district." School board members also may have to choose between "someone who's done the work as superintendent, or an individual who is on their way up."

A well-done search can last between three and six months, but even then, Holcomb advises board members not to settle on any candidate they have doubts about. "Go back out and search some more," she said. "I no longer put deadlines on applications because you never know what's going to happen. Continue searching until you have a successful candidate."

BEYOND DEBATES: TALKING TOGETHER ABOUT STUDENT ACHIEVEMENT

Another district that has benefited from a long collaborative relationship between its school board and superintendent is Springdale, Arkansas. At the end of a long interview about its board practices, board member Kathy McFetridge got to the heart of the matter: "I have to say, we have the best superintendent you could possibly want. He's been with us twenty-seven years. He communicates well with us and treats us with respect, doesn't show any favoritism, and, in turn, has the real support of the board. We go out with a unanimous vote every time."

The second-largest school district in Arkansas, Springdale is a growing community with a burgeoning Hispanic population. It's headquarters to Tyson Foods Inc. and twenty miles from Bentonville, headquarters of Wal-Mart. The school district is grappling not only with rapid growth in enrollment (ten new schools were built in the last six years), but also with increasing numbers of English language learners. In response, the superintendent has implemented, among other things, a professional development program in adolescent literacy for twelve-hundred teachers, a Toyota Family Literacy Program, an English language academy for high schoolers, and ninth- and tenth-grade language centers in the high schools, with four core teachers assigned to each. "There are a lot of students and lots of ways for those students to get lost if we're not careful," said McFetridge.

In addition to test scores, the board is watching dropout rates carefully and is seeing steady progress in keeping students in school. The school board was also the first in the state to require students to earn four math credits for high school graduation. According to the super-intendent, Jim Rollins, more Springdale graduates qualify for college scholarships than graduates in any other district in the state.

With Rollins, the board participates in three all-day work sessions a year to "brainstorm about the vision for the district and new prac-tices," go over data, and talk with principals and teachers invited by the superintendent. "It opens communication channels, which helps dur-ing the year," said McFetridge. Conflicts are rare. "When you stay fo-cused on the children and you can put your issues aside, you don't have conflict," she said. "We usually talk things out in a board meeting. The board works hard to look supportive of the system. There's confidence in the school system because of that. We don't have anyone who has any other agenda but the kids."

Springdale superintendent Rollins credits an internal communication system created twenty years ago for helping to sustain a collaborative board–superintendent relationship in the district. Each month, he or his deputy meets "to talk school" and get input from three different groups made up of representatives from the twenty-six school PTAs, school build-ing staff, and support staff. New ideas—whether they involve school finance, curriculum, school uniforms, or parent involvement—are "pro-cessed to the hilt," he said. "In all honesty, I don't think there's a policy issue of any significance at all that has gone to our board for decision mak-ing in the last twenty years that hasn't been dealt with in that manner. When you bring a recommendation before the board with that kind of col-lective input, there really isn't much to argue about," he continued.

He gives his board credit for helping to "grow a culture where every-one is trying to do the very best for our kids.

"We work together in a spirit of mutual respect. We identify the com-mon ground constantly. The focus is on the kids, and we try to engage partners to help us whenever we can," he said. "Whatever quality exists in a school district begins and ends with the school board. The board sets the tone so the entire staff can do their work. The board gives me the confidence, and sets the boundaries, and lets us serve. We can't do it effectively by doing it apart."

Board members may be politicians who must run for reelection from time to time, but not many high-functioning boards put a premium on political debates at the board table. For one thing, it looks too much like the type of fighting that signals lack of collaboration. Lack of collaboration begets loss of confidence from the public, which can translate into lack of votes in favor of raising school levies and other forms of support for public schools.

Local newspaper reporters and reality TV buffs may enjoy a good fight between board members, but it doesn't do anyone else much good, especially the students of the district. In fact, many boards are cutting back on formal decision-making meetings in front of the camera in favor of the kind of longer informational meetings that foster serious conversations about student achievement like those in Springdale. The kinds of issues and solutions these boards and superintendents talk about—formative assessment, "fingertip" assessments, data management systems—are just too complex to sum up in sound bites.

Another reason may be that boards and superintendents are entering new territory when they talk in detail about student achievement. It's clear that even high-functioning boards are still feeling their way. Mary Delagardelle made that point at the 2008 NSBA convention. When the Lighthouse Project began training the pilot districts in practices associated with "moving boards" in phase 2 of the research project, board members were the most nervous about the idea of connecting more with district-level leadership around issues relating to teaching and learning. "They were worried about crossing that sacred line," she told conference attendees, referring to the traditional demarcation between the overseer role of the board and the day-to-day management of the superintendent.

Board members were able to overcome this anxiety once they became convinced that they had educational responsibilities that could not be abdicated, explained Delagardelle later, in an interview. "Their focus [as a board] is on the outcomes and what they want to accomplish, while the [superintendent's] job is about how are we going to meet those expectations and to explain the plan. Because the board is going to have to fund it and explain it. It wasn't about micromanaging. It was about an important policy role that nobody was going to play, if they weren't going to play it."

Adding to the potential role confusion is the fact that "nobody understands the role of the board," she said. "The community expects them to be their advocates in things that they don't like; superintendents put them in a cabinet role because they don't want to make decisions alone."

Board members are neither passive agents of the superintendent nor professional educators, says Delagardelle. To help the boards keep perspective, the Lighthouse researchers worked with boards to identify five roles, and kept referring to them when questions about roles and responsibilities came up (see figure 2.2).

"There is no one leading [school improvement] work who's not in the trenches, except the board," Delagardelle continued. "When they could see their role as part of a leadership continuum, they began to understand that if they didn't play the policy-making role, no one else would. The superintendent could; until there is controversy, and then if you haven't brought your board along, the superintendent is left in the lurch. The board is the only one who can stay on the balcony all the time and be that pressure and support so that when things get hard, they can move it forward."

Even high-functioning boards are still working this arrangement out. "The line" is now more fluid. One member, speaking confidentially, told this story to illustrate the dilemma: "We were setting the agenda, and we were talking about the data retreat and how much to go into it, and the superintendent's response was, 'That is micromanaging,'" said the member. "It used to be considered that, but now it's more about understanding. We need to find out where these gaps are and what we need to do to improve. We look at the overall picture, and once we see the overall picture,

FIGURE 2.2 *Five roles of a school board*

- Set clear expectations for outcomes of district improvement work.
- Hold the board and staff accountable for meeting the expectations.
- Create conditions for success.
- Build the collective will to succeed.
- Learn together as a board team.

Source: Mary Delagardelle, "The Lighthouse Inquiry: Examining the Role of School Board Leadership in the Improvement of Student Achievement," in *The Future of School Board Governance: Relevancy and Revelation,* ed. Thomas L. Alsbury (Lanham, MD: Rowman & Littlefield Education, 2008).

we need to talk to them and say, 'How are you going to improve this?' It's up to them to look in much more detail. The integrity of that process gives me the assurance as a board member that we are working hard as a district to improve achievement." By the time they got to the retreat, however, the superintendent had changed his mind. "The superintendent actually brought it up first, and he said, 'I rethought my conclusion,'" said the member, adding, "It's just something we have to work though."

Conversations centered on real investigations into student outcomes tend to bring both parties—boards and superintendents—together. One important clue as to whether this is happening is to listen to the words that board members and superintendents use to describe their working relationship. In one district in this book, a superintendent calls his board "an educational family." In another, the superintendent is called the "tenth board member." Clearly, "the line" is blurring.

COMMIT TO CHANGE

Superintendents have a hard time collaborating with boards that don't back them up, especially after they've approved a difficult change that holds promise for students. Good superintendents also don't necessarily stick around to work with waffling boards, either. Conversely, superintendents who are empowered by boards can get a lot done. Implicit, then, in the concept of collaboration is solidarity or commitment, especially in the face of resistance to agreed-upon change.

What happened in Madison County, Kentucky, illustrates the benefits of commitment by a board. In 2005, the school board and then-superintendent Mike Caudill accepted an invitation by the state department of education to participate in its Voluntary Partnership Assistance Team (VPAT). Both parties were unhappy with the student performance on the state tests and disturbed by the difference in scores among subgroups. "We looked at the subgroup [scores] and thought that, despite our best efforts, something wasn't working," remembered Doug Whitlock, board chairman. As part of the program, the state would perform a scholastic audit of the school system. "Mike came to us, as a board, to say this was an opportunity; it would expose our warts to the world, but he thought it was the right thing to do," said Whitlock. "We went in with the attitude that even if it made us uncomfortable, we were comfortable with being uncomfortable."

The state findings revealed deficiencies in eight major areas, including what the audit called "lack of urgency about student achievement within the district leadership," according to Whitlock.

In the 1990s, Kentucky had placed much of the responsibility for school reform decisions with school-based councils. District school boards became more "business, financial, and construction oriented," and the boards' role in student achievement was limited, explained Whitlock, who has watched school reform play out from his dual roles on the Madison County school board and as president of Eastern Kentucky University. "We have some individual schools that are truly outstanding and that probably gave us a little sense of complacency, but you don't have to be a low-achieving district to be placed in Tier three," said Whitlock, referring to the labeled used in Kentucky for districts that fail to make AYP four years in a row.

It would have been easy to go into denial as a result of the state audit finding, he said, but the board did not. Instead, it adopted the audit's recommendations, including one advising the board to do a better job of communicating its commitment to improving student achievement. District administration was reorganized by Caudill, and an academic officer was hired to help principals become instructional leaders rather than managers. The chief academic officer, Tommy Floyd, instituted new student assessments as well as classroom walkthroughs to monitor teaching practices. Teachers were organized into teams, or professional learning communities, that met periodically to analyze student data and brainstorm ways for helping students make more progress. Individual student intervention plans were made for "Mike's Kids," or struggling students. A VPAT team of mentors and experts provided by the state began visiting individual schools to offer guidance. Whitlock, as a board chairman, participated on the VPAT team to send a message about the board's commitment to student achievement and to communicate progress to the rest of the board. The board also attended joint training with principals in the summers and injected more accountability into its policy making. Every recommendation for a new initiative must "close the loop" to include a date by which the board will receive a report evaluating its effectiveness.

The board changed the focus and tenure of its meetings, said Whitlock. "We are much more outcome oriented. If we're talking about out-of-state field trips, questions [in the past] would be, 'Do you have enough chaperones?' Now it's, how many days of instruction are going to be missed, how will they be made up? How does this fit with the curriculum?

But the district's new focus on achievement didn't sit well with everyone. "We've had plenty of people call us as individuals and say, 'Make it stop,'" said Whitlock. "When you institutionalize walkthroughs, when you set the expectation that there will be formative assessment, people's lives are affected. We just had to show resolve as a board and [not] allow [ourselves] to be fragmented." The district made AYP after the first year, and the calls stopped, he said. "People have seen the intervention and the professional development that we've done, and that things are working. Nothing makes people buy in more quickly than something like that."

For Floyd, the board's attitude made all the difference. "It was almost like there was existing potential that existed, but what it took was our board making the decision that student achievement would be what they focused on, period. We had some resistance, but the board said, 'I'm very sorry, but student achievement is number one.' Everything from that point on enabled the superintendent and everybody else to focus on that." Floyd, who succeeded Caudill as superintendent in 2008 after Caudill passed away from cancer, still remembers Caudill urging him on in his new job as chief academic officer to start making changes, saying, "Son, just go, the board's behind it, so let's go."

Floyd calls his board "an educational family." "I keep them very, very informed, and send an e-mail every Friday that details what I did all week. And I call them." If a member gets sidetracked by an issue not related to district priorities, "one of my five will bring them back," he said.

Now, four years after the VPAT team began its work, the district has met AYP in all categories, and elementary school achievement is above state and national norms, said Whitlock. "One good thing that has come to the district as a result of No Child Left Behind is the rediscovery of the fact that school boards have a role to play in student achievement," he added. Although the district is out of Tier 3 status, the VPAT team continues to make the rounds of the schools.

Because of the positive experience in Madison County, the state is now recommending that board members be part of the newly expanded VPAT process, called ASSIST (Assist and Support School Improvement Success Teams), for districts that have failed to make AYP for two or more years. (The state also contracts with the state board association to find former board members to mentor board members in districts referred for the ASSIST process.) "The strength of that board, which I would hold up as a standard for state boards, is that they allowed the improvement process to become part of its culture," said David Cook, policy adviser with the Office of Leadership and School Improvement at the Kentucky Department of Education. "I don't foresee worrying about them sustaining the improvement, because they have changed the way they do things. What I like about going to a board meeting in Madison County is, a good chunk of the meeting is about the students or teachers and talking about what they are doing."

A board's resolve to stick with a promising educational initiative can be a real tipping point for a district, as was also the case of Laurens District 55 in South Carolina.

In 1994, Laurens had hired a strong, promising superintendent in Ed Taylor, but there was conflict and lack of trust on the board, said Leni Patterson, board member and former chair. Patterson, who describes herself as a "committed community service" volunteer and mother of three, and who is also the admissions dean at Presbyterian College, attended school board meetings for about a year before she threw her hat in the ring. "A longtime member retired, so I ran to get on the board and focus on what was needed and to not nitpick," she said.

"The superintendent had done some innovative things previously in a small district; he had implemented a Montessori program, for example. And when he first came to Laurens, at one of the meetings he put forth a vision of about twenty things. I just really liked what he had in mind. They were stretches for us," said Patterson.

Among the initiatives the superintendent put in place was a plan for moving some teachers, including one veteran teacher, to a new community school with a novice staff. "She was a very, very good teacher," said Patterson. "They needed her talents, and that was the motivation for moving her. It was about what was good for kids." The teacher's colleagues at the old school began calling board members in protest.

Although it was his decision to make, the superintendent had briefed the Laurens board about his decision and his reasons ahead of time. Board members repeated the rationale for the change to those who called them. "The board's response was, we're doing this because we believe it is best for children," recalls Patterson. "Each and every board member said the same thing to callers. And the phone calls stopped. I see that as a real turning point in the district, when the teachers realized the board was going to do right by kids."

It was also a good example of the kind of communication that inspires collaboration between superintendents and boards, she said, because the superintendent came to the board and presented the plan for moving teachers before implementing it. "He knew there would be some discourse, so before the phone calls started, he had prepped us."

"As long as there is really strong communication from both sides, it leads to the ability to have more trust," said Patterson.

BEWARE OF BACKLASH: THE DOWNSIDE OF COLLABORATION

The public tends to notice when boards work well with their superintendents, especially if previous board–superintendent teams were marked by overt conflict. Since a lot of collaboration occurs informally at work sessions or between meetings between individual board members and the superintendent, what the public sees at meetings in person or on cable television is a lot of agreement resulting in mostly unanimous votes. Boards run the risk of being labeled as rubber stamps.

For this reason, while it is important to collaborate, it's also important to keep a healthy distance. Board members serve as representatives of their locality and on behalf of the students the district serves. They have two masters: the inner, specialized world of schools and the outer world of the community, which may know little of what is really going on inside the schools. One way some board members do this is to envision themselves as a bridge between these two worlds.

Superintendents can help a collaborative board fulfill its civic responsibilities by accommodating (within reason) board requests for the information needed to make an informed decision and defend it in public.

"Make sure that you are engaged," advises Patterson. "It's not about just showing up once a month. Keep up with information that the superintendent provides. Keep asking good questions."

Superintendents need to give board members credit for wanting that information, too, says Patterson. "We have people who are very strong and intelligent on our board. Sometimes [the superintendent] doesn't give us enough information, and we'll say, 'We don't have enough information. We don't want to do this yet.' It all boils down to communication. We haven't told him no, but we have asked for additional information before making a decision. We don't want to be taken advantage of, because we have been so supportive."

CHAPTER THREE

Staying Focused on Achievement

Meeting Setting Goals Using Data

BERLIN, CT • NORFOLK, VA • BOSTON, MA • LA CROSSE, WI

Few would argue that the field of education has become increasingly complex, touching on many different disciplines and subjects, including pedagogy, curriculum, management, psychology, psychometrics (testing), neuroscience—just to name a few. Much of this may be familiar ground for superintendents with doctorate degrees, but that's not necessarily the case for many school board members. The job has evolved by quantum leaps since the early days of picking an able schoolmaster and ordering wood.

It's a tricky balancing act. Board members need to know enough about the work of educators seeking to raise achievement to be able to assess their efforts, support them, and communicate about them, without dictating what should be done. They need to have enough information to make good decisions without being overwhelmed.

Maintaining a focus on achievement is another challenge. School board meetings serve many purposes at once: to get the "regular" business done, including the passing of mandated state and federal policies and a myriad of other duties laid out by state laws; to deliberate on new policies; to pass the budget; to evaluate the superintendent; and to hear input from the public on any number of topics.

As part of their new role, it's clear that high-functioning boards are restructuring meetings for new purposes, setting goals to focus the work of the district, and asking for the kind of data that can help them in their role as policy makers.

USING MEETINGS STRATEGICALLY

It makes sense that if school boards are serious about student achievement, anyone watching their meetings should be able to tell. "If student achievement is at the top of the list, meetings should reflect that," said Gary Brochu, board president in Berlin, Connecticut, a suburb outside Hartford. A school law attorney, Brochu calls himself a "missionary for what we are trying to accomplish in our schools." "In no other volunteer work that I do, do I take an oath," he said.

Before beginning each meeting, Brochu recites the district's mission statement: "The board of education is committed to supporting continuous improvement leading to student achievement and student success." Then he adds, "I hope this meeting is one more step in that process."

"It may seem like a little thing," said Berlin superintendent Michael Cicchetti, "but over time, the administration, the staff, and the community hear the same thing, and it sinks in. It's as relentless as our continuous efforts in the district."

"We have twenty-one regular formal meetings a year," Brochu explained. "It's not that many. The way I look at it, each board year, you should be telling a story, like writing a novel, and each meeting should be a chapter. It's our limited chance to tell what we think is important to the community. If your meetings are focused on trivia, that's what the community will think of your work. That message also gets to staff. You can't expect the community to believe that you are focused on student achievement if your meetings are about something else. Boards have extraordinary power that is not tapped into."

It all started in 2004, when the nine-member Berlin board decided to use the occasion of a change in superintendents and the arrival of a few new board members to set out its priorities for the future. Members started with a weekend retreat. Cicchetti helped them plan it and found a consultant to help. The board, in consultation with Cicchetti, came up with four new goals, with indicators to measure progress. The board abolished its old subcommittees and set up three to match the new goals (see figure 3.1).

Members also reworked the format of the board's meeting agenda in collaboration with Cicchetti. Everything on their regular business meeting agenda appears under one consent agenda, meaning a number of routine matters can be dispensed with in one vote. Every meeting includes one or two presentations by the administration that relate to teaching and learning. "We are not talking about voting for field trips

FIGURE 3.1   *Aligning subcommittees with goals in Berlin, CT*

Committee	Goals and indicators
Leadership, accountability, and measurement	Each and every student in the Berlin Public Schools will achieve established, rigorous performance standards in all areas of student learning by becoming independent strategic readers, problem solvers, and critical thinkers.
	Students in grades 5, 8, and 10 meeting goal in reading, writing, mathematics, and science through the Connecticut Mastery Test and Connecticut Academic Performance Test.
	High school graduate rate through a cohort comparison of students who enter in grade 9 and graduate in grade 12.
	Survey of high school graduates five years from graduation to determine their status and preparedness related to college and career.
Communications and alignment	The Berlin Board of Education will establish reciprocal communication that is accessible and understandable, and that unites all citizens around the belief that high-quality public education is a community's most valuable asset.
	Number of people accessing the Berlin Public Schools Web site and utilizing the e-mail option to share information or ask questions.
	Number of nonparents who come to the schools to volunteer or attend events.
	Accessibility of BOE meetings to the public.
	Survey of Berlin residents regarding the effectiveness of communication efforts.
	Survey of new residents to determine what role the quality of the public schools played in their decision to move to Berlin.

(continued)

FIGURE 3.1 *(continued)*

Committee	Goals and indicators
Resources and capacity building	The Berlin Board of Education will ensure all students have the opportunity to learn and achieve in safe and educationally adequate facilities by meeting the needs of the district with respect to adequate space and the quality of learning environments.
	Educational adequacy: Based on criteria used in the NESDEC Facilities study, the educational space at each school will be identified as "adequate" or "inadequate," and a percentage determined for individual schools and the district.
	NEASC accreditation report findings for Berlin high school and how the facilities or safety-related recommendations are addressed.
	Safety: Fire Marshal develops and conducts an audit of all schools yearly and makes recommendation. Progress is measured from year to year as to how recommendations are addressed.
	Police Department develops and conducts safety/security audit of all schools and makes recommendations. Progress is measured from year to year as to how recommendations are addressed.
	Evidence, available resources, and timeliness of the district's proactive measures as well as the district's response to health and safety-related issues.

Source: Berlin Public Schools.

. . . we don't even want to talk about that stuff. We want to talk about what we are doing K–8 in math curriculum," said Brochu.

There is also a place on each meeting's agenda for board members and department heads alike to give a quick forty-five-second update on what they've been doing since the last meeting. Both board members and the public get a better idea of all the work that is being done. Small doses, big impact is the idea, said Cicchetti, who Brochu calls "the tenth board member."

The Berlin board, an elected board, also has a line item in the school budget to pay for professional development requested by board members. "It is our expectation that our board members will invest in their own development," said Brochu. "If there's an opportunity to loop the board in with staff, in curriculum training, then we will do it." At a full-day workshop for staff on twenty-first-century skills, for example, the board came in and listened for two hours. It doesn't mean the board gets involved with how curriculum is designed, Brochu said. In this respect, they observe "the line."

But board members have to know enough to be "partners in the conversation," he said. "You have to be able to understand what quality teaching and rigor mean, and the difference between the tests. I think it's essential that you can have that conversation."

INFORMAL MEETINGS AND GOAL SETTING

Regular meetings have their limits, though. They are not good formats for discussing complicated issues (like the differences between tests), and they typically happen in the evening after work when board members, many of whom also have full-time jobs, are tired.

Within the limits imposed by sunshine laws—those that require boards to do most kinds of business in legally posted meetings— effective school boards use a wide array of meeting formats. Often, the purpose is to find time to craft goals, study data, or understand new initiatives relating to student achievement. These meetings include workshops, work sessions, annual retreats, and off-site meetings.

In Norfolk, Virginia, for example, the board participates in several different types of meetings in the course of one regular monthly board meeting. "The first hour is personnel," explained Barry Bishop, the board chair. "Then, two hours of an informational meeting. We might get two to three reports then. We sit around a conference table. That's the best place to have a conversation with our leadership team. That's the richest part of the meeting. At seven is the formal meeting. All the board members are up on the dais, and that's not so conducive to conversation. Then we have once a month, sometimes more, a work session—a couple of hours where we really drill in on something particular." The Norfolk board also has an annual retreat in January to set goals.

One of the most important board meetings typically happens at the goal-setting retreat. Annual goals are typically used as the basis for longer-range strategic plans crafted by the superintendent with targets (or "benchmarks") periodically monitored by the board. These are also typically used as the basis of the superintendent's annual evaluation.

Goals are also the vehicle whereby high-functioning boards can raise expectations for learning in their communities. Collaborating on goals with the superintendent is common on high-functioning boards; although just who starts the ball rolling—the superintendent or the board—can vary.

Bishop credits the success of the Norfolk district—it won the Broad Prize for Urban Education in 2005—to "a consistent, unrelenting focus on the overarching goals of the district."

In 2000, the board decided on three objectives that center on increasing achievement for all students, creating a safe learning environment, and fostering community involvement (see box 3.1). Members have stuck with them since, he said. The district also has an annual accountability system, tied to the three objectives, and meeting agenda items also relate. In addition to tracking progress on state and local achievement measures, school principals choose seven indicators to chart progress in their buildings toward each of the three objectives. The accountability system helps the board "decide what works so we can replicate it or stop doing it," Bishop said.

BOX 3.1

Norfolk Goals and Objectives

The school board of the City of Norfolk has set one goal for the district:

- Improving the quality of teaching and learning for *all* . . . *all* means *all*.

    As part of our efforts to achieve this goal, we align our work with three key objectives:

- To ensure the continuous growth of student academic achievement for *all* . . . *all* means *all*.

- To ensure that each school provides a safe, secure, and disciplined teaching and learning environment.

- To ensure that parents, businesses, and community members are actively engaged in the educational process.

Source: Norfolk School Board (VA).

Having a long-term commitment to the same set of goals helped weather a critical period after the abrupt retirement of their superintendent in 2004, said Bishop. "We made it very, very clear that we were simply not going to use the excuse of his leaving for things to stop moving. We made it clear that we were on the right road. It is so important that what you are doing becomes part of the culture. It can't ride on one individual," he said.

The board hasn't always been as focused, Bishop said. "One of my very first meetings was the annual retreat in 1999. In those days, a successful meeting used to be [measured by] how many 3M posters were being put up. Now, we don't have a plan-a-month. There's something to be said for staying the course."

Norfolk is one of the districts that has partnered with the Panasonic Foundation for systemic reform. The board's annual retreats are facilitated by the Panasonic Foundation and are complemented by regular off-site meetings for board and district representatives, also sponsored by Panasonic, to focus on three achievable results for the year, which are related to the district's larger objectives.

An appointed board, Norfolk, too, has had to confront "the line." As chair, Bishop has to arbitrate requests from board members for more information from the administration. "We don't want individual board members asking for information that takes people off task. If it's readily available, the administration just shares it. If it's something they are going to have to mine a lot of information for, then I determine the interest level of the other members. Sometimes it's just as important what a board doesn't do. Our job is policy, not to direct or run the school district, [but] we aren't perfect in that regard."

One of the Norfolk board's four "Established Norms of Interaction" states, "We will maintain open communication with each other and the administration."[1] As part of this norm, all information requests of the administration are to be sent to the superintendent through the board chair. If "considerable work or time is required to generate the data, the full board must endorse the request," the policy states. The other three Norfolk norms require that all board members speak "candidly and courteously," listening to dissenting voices with an open mind, ultimately supporting the final decision of the board "in word and deed";

respect the different roles played by those in the district and concentrate on governing through policy, referring problems to the superintendent to solve; and focus on the development and monitoring of an annual accountability plan while sustaining a "climate of trust."

Andrew Gelber, a senior consultant with the Panasonic Foundation, calls the Norfolk board "quite sophisticated."

PUTTING THE LITTLE *P* IN POLITICS: AN ENGAGED CHAIR

As Bishop illustrates, chairs (or presidents) of high-functioning boards are fully involved and engaged in facilitating collaboration, as well as policing agreed-upon ways of operating. They are often the point person for representing the rest of the board in working with the superintendent to set meeting agendas and for speaking as the "voice" of the board with the media and others.

Informally, they can play a critical role in anticipating and managing conflict between board members and between individual members and the superintendent. Typically, they are more experienced members of the board, so they are usually in a good position to know who is sensitive to what on the board and in the community, and, therefore, what kind of changes will be easy or hard, requiring a longer process or a different process to accomplish the desired goal. Since they run the actual board meetings and help determine meeting agendas, their talents often determine whether a board is seen as efficient at doing the district's business or not. In the 1997 NESDEC study, researchers singled out effective board chair communication as "vital to the effectiveness of the superintendent and the board."[2]

Not every board member is willing or able to play this important diplomatic role. For this reason, NESDEC and other governance experts recommend that board members elect their own chairs, rather than rotating or allowing other bodies (selectmen, city councilors, mayors) to choose them.

In Boston, which won the Broad Prize the year after Norfolk, the appointed committee (in Massachusetts, school boards are called *school committees*) elects its own chair every year. Board member Elizabeth Reilinger, who served as chair for twelve years, likens the chair's role to that of a "coach." "I can say to the superintendent, you know this is-sue is going to be of considerable concern to X and Y on the board, so it might merit it that you sit down or talk with [other members] on the phone so you can explain what you are confronting and [ask] what's their input and direction," she said. "Sometimes I suggested that we float some preliminary set of thoughts, not even a recommendation. You have to help the superintendent understand that while what they may want to do makes sense in a vacuum, they are not in a vacuum."

For example, when a school consolidation plan proposed by the ad-ministration ran into community opposition, Reilinger suggested break-ing up the proposal rather than offering it as a whole package, to get the no-brainers off the table and allow committee members to focus on solving the more difficult pieces.

Other practices adopted by the board, and monitored by the chair, help to keep the discussion moving efficiently, she said. Meeting agen-das are carefully crafted by the superintendent and the board chair in six-month segments. Meetings are kept to two hours in length, and in-formation is sent to the committee the Friday prior to the Wednesday meeting, to allow adequate time for questions and clarifications from members. In addition to a small consent agenda for routine matters, each meeting features two to three reports on something pertaining to the district's priorities. Rather than having standing subcommittees, the committee makes use of ad hoc task forces to make recommendations on a specific policy issue, like changes to the student assignment plan. As chair, Reilinger said she encouraged members to talk to the super-intendent first before contacting staff, and intervened, if necessary, to make sure members didn't step overstep into the management role. A good chair understands the role of a governing board and actively man-ages the board, she said.

Reilinger says the Boston board has been able to help raise student achievement by staying focused on important policy and financial deci-sions and setting priorities with the superintendent, and that this was made possible because in 1993 it switched from being an elected board to one where members were appointed by the mayor. "What that in es-sence did, was to change the dynamic from political with a capital P political agenda, to a small p," she said. "We got people [to focus on a] discussion about academics and the issue of student achievement. While structure is never fully the answer, it has a great deal with whether it advances the discussion or impedes it." However, as the examples in this book show, both elected and appointed boards are establishing policies and procedures to put "the little *p*" in board business by defining roles, policies, and other procedures that enable them to keep the priority on student achievement.

Chairs often play their most critical role in those gray areas in board–superintendent relationships that are subject to interpretation or individual preference. For example, it is generally agreed that the superintendent is responsible for getting enough information to school boards to allow them to make a policy or budget decision or evaluate the superintendent. What a member needs, or thinks they need, however, can vary quite a bit from one member to another. How much information should an individual member be able to request? Are they using information requests on a fishing expedition to find problems, or out of genuine need for help in making a decision? As in Norfolk, it often falls to the chair to mediate. Without a strong chair committed to helping to move things along, boards can get stuck on minor issues.

FOCUSING ON ENDS WITH POLICY GOVERNANCE

What if you don't have a strong chair or don't want to depend on one for staying on task? Some boards that seek a more formal way of staying focused on student achievement have turned to a program called "Policy Governance," designed originally for use by corporate boards and trademarked by former CEO John Carver, a board consultant, author, and adjunct professor at the Institute for Nonprofit Organizations at the University of Georgia, Athens.

As practiced by school boards, this governance model has four simple features. A board first agrees to a statement on those things that the chief executive (or superintendent) cannot do, called *executive limitations*. The board then settles on a number of goals, called *ends policies*, that the superintendent is going to work on and upon which he or she will be evaluated. The school board declares that the superintendent is its only employee, and empowers him or her to do anything to achieve the goals, except what is prohibited by the executive limitations. Periodically, the board must meet with groups in the community, called *linkages*, as part of an ongoing process of revising or establishing new end goals. The superintendent submits monitoring reports on progress toward the goals, which are used for his or her evaluation.

In 2000, the La Crosse, Wisconsin, school board adopted what it calls *governance by policy*. Board president Christine Clair, a former criminal defense attorney who was elected the year the board began to implement the policy governance model, said the board was drawn to it because "without having their policies aligned with student achievement, it was too easy to get distracted and go down another road." With a consultant, the board spent two full weekend retreats developing a district vision and three ends policies around academic achievement and promoting citizenship and "responsible life choices" (see figure 3.2). "The policies are really short and sweet, but we had a lot of philosophical discussions to get to them, said Clair. "We felt there were so many different ways of measuring student achievement, we didn't just want to look at test scores," she explained. The board has since modified the model slightly to add more frequent interim monitoring reports from the superintendent, Clair said.

The board also worked with the superintendent to develop a school profile system as another way of monitoring progress toward the goals. In addition to testing and other data, schools are given the leeway to pick their own activities to make progress toward three end goals. For example, schools choose how they will work with students to increase community involvement (ends goal 3) and also report the number of students who participated broken down by grade level and subgroup in separate documents. (See appendix A, "La Crosse School Profile.")

"Ends policies are kind of like the gospel; we tell the superintendent what he can't do, then he and his staff are able to do anything else to achieve our ends policies," said Clair. "We've done this because we know we are not the educational experts. We want to give the superintendent the ability to be creative to come up with the best educational programs, but he has to prove to us that what he does is working." Clair said the board has a good relationship with the superintendent because of this governance system. "We allow him the flexibility to use the collective resources of his staff, and we don't tie his hands," she said.

FIGURE 3.2 *La Crosse, Wisconsin, ends policies*

E-I
District Vision

Students will discover their talents and abilities and will be prepared to pursue their dreams and aspirations while contributing effectively to their local, national, and global communities.

E-2
Academic Achievement Goals

Students will demonstrate continuous improvement toward a high level of individual success in all required and elective academic/curricular areas using multiple measures of performance.

1. Students will:
   a. Meet achievable and developmentally appropriate goals through collaborative planning with their teachers and parents/caregivers.
   b. Achieve clearly defined competence or mastery in all curricular areas as monitored by an array of quantitative and qualitative measures.
   c. Develop higher-order critical-thinking skills.
   d. Develop and exercise creativity in problem solving and self-expression.
   e. Develop the curiosity, self-discipline, and self-awareness necessary for life-long learning.
2. Students will show continuous improvement through multiple measures of the K–12 reading, mathematics, science, and social studies programs.

E-3
Involved Citizenship

Students will strive for mutual understanding as contributing citizens in a diverse world and global community.

Policy governance has helped keep the board focused on student achievement, she said, which is important because the community of only seven thousand students has seen an influx of English language learners, and 40 percent of the student population now qualifies for free or reduced lunch.

Students will:

1. Understand and exercise the rights and responsibilities of citizenship in our democratic society.

2. Volunteer time and talents.

3. Practice the shared community values of honesty, respect, responsibility, compassion, self-discipline, perseverance, and giving.

4. Clarify personal values and effectively use them in relationships.

5. Utilize critical thinking and content knowledge necessary to appreciate cultural and individual differences.

6. Demonstrate effective skills in team as well as individual endeavors.

7. Demonstrate effective and comprehensive communication skills.

8. Practice good stewardship toward the environment.

9. Develop a worldview for mutual understanding.

E-4
Responsible Life Choices

Students will acquire the knowledge and skills necessary to make effective and responsible life choices.

Students will:

1. Apply critical-thinking and problem-solving skills.

2. Demonstrate creativity and innovation.

3. Show courage and commitment to their choices, values, and beliefs.

4. Understand the dynamics of change and possess coping and resiliency skills.

5. Establish good health and wellness practices.

6. Successfully manage personal resources.

Source: School District of La Crosse.

"Everyone is committed to trying to keep student achievement in the forefront, and because of that we are able to keep going forward," Clair said. "We have disputes and such, but we don't have any way of getting off-track; if we do, it gets called, and someone says, how is this related to student achievement? We don't get into what kind of floor should we put in the gym, or if we should put a pool into a school, because Northside wants it. We don't get into that."

The board has established sixteen ELs, or executive limitations, the most recent requiring the superintendent to get board approval before closing any facility. "When you know what you can't do, and that you can do everything else, it's actually freeing," said superintendent Gerald Kember. When in doubt, he will call Clair, the board chair, who will say, "I don't think that's an EL, so go ahead." At meetings, "whenever a conversation gets off the ends policy, [board members] will challenge each other," said Kember. "They will say, 'I think we are getting into the work of our administrative team.'"

Another benefit, he said, is that the board can keep its policies more up-to-date since there are fewer to keep up with. "Before governance, we had a policy book that was five inches thick. There were policies about everything that you can imagine, like when a student is sick, at what point does a student have to bring in a doctor's note to get back into school? Really administrative stuff. We had a heck of a time updating it."

When the board established the vision and ends policies, along with the executive limitations and its own operating rules (called *governance process*, or *GPs*, and board/superintendent relationship, or *BSRs*), "all the nitty-gritty went into administrative policy," said Kember, adding, "Now that the board has a manageable number of policies, each is on an annual schedule for being monitored." In addition, the board has only four committees relating to its major responsibilities: a governance committee for vetting policy revisions and scheduling linkages with community groups, a legislative committee for following education policy at the state and federal levels, a communications committee for community outreach, and an executive committee made up of officers of the board.

The change in governance by the elected board "is allowing the community to say what it wants for its schools and children, but at the same time putting the daily decision making in the hands of the professionals," said Kember. Despite the changing demographics in the district, La Crosse is one of the few in the state where all its schools are making AYP, he said.

The only distractions have been the five funding referendums the district has had to seek for its schools since 2004, said Clair. Two referendums in 2004 and 2008 were needed to raise taxes over revenue limits in order to cover operating expenses for things like the district's priority to maintain small class sizes for grades K–3, which are not fully funded by the state. The district also has old buildings and sought a capital referendum in 2008 as well for critical maintenance projects, such as repairs to boilers originally installed in 1938. "The referendums have taken just a huge amount of time, energy, and [attention] from the board and the district administration and staff when we could be working more on student achievement," said Clair. The board had meetings with more than 120 community groups to explain the need for the tax overrides. Since the last two referendums passed, "we're happy campers now," said Clair, of the board. "The last board meeting, it was just great; we could talk about the reading report."

Whether it is through a model like policy governance or a homegrown policy and meeting framework collaboratively arrived at, high-functioning school boards find a way to focus, and maintain the focus, on student achievement.

MONITORING WITH DATA: DON'T BE A DRIP

As you have probably figured out by now, data is an important component in the work of high-functioning boards. Good data is needed not only for accountability purposes and for monitoring student achievement, but also to better understand the need for initiatives recommended by the superintendent so board members can lend their support, particularly at budget time.

In the age of accountability—where educators are looking at and comparing results of classroom, district, state, national, and even international assessments—there is no shortage of data to be had. The real challenge for school boards and superintendents is to figure out what kind of data the board needs to fulfill its governance role. Those who work with school boards to set up accountability, monitoring, and evaluation plans say boards need to use different sets of data than others working in a district to keep an eye on the big picture. Failure to make this distinction can lead to what's often referred to as DRIP (data rich/information poor).[3]

When I interviewed the chair of the Boston School Committee late in 2008, the committee was wrestling with this very issue. Reilinger said the district was looking at data points under previous whole school reform initiatives and trying to decide what to track. "Some are redundant," she said. "You don't want to get into the data overload situation. We're clear about the summative (the state MCAS tests), but do we have the right formative assessments? We are struggling to get the right formative assessments, [but] you don't want the board getting into the discussion of every quarterly result. That's like watching the stock market . . . The important thing is getting staff real-time data so they can act on it. The board's role is to make sure it's in place."

Under the leadership of longtime superintendent Thomas Payzant, the district made the use of data a central feature in its plans to improve teaching and learning and student outcomes.[4] This emphasis has continued under Carol Johnson, who succeeded Payzant following his retirement in 2006. In September 2008, Johnson presented an accelerated learning plan to the Boston School Committee, with eight goals to guide student achievement through 2012, including goals for first- and third-grade reading, fifth- and seventh-grade writing, eighth-grade math, tenth-grade pass rates on Massachusetts's state tests, twelfth-grade SAT scores, proficiency scores for English language learners, and dropout and graduation rates.

The plan, called Charting the Course to Excellence, couldn't be easier to read. One page is devoted to each goal, and each contains a short problem statement, one or two sentences summarizing the performance history in each area, and numerical targets for each of the four academic years 2009 through 2012. (See figure 3.3.) Some targets will rely on existing assessments, like the SAT; some will require the district to develop new ones, like a common writing assessment for fifth and seventh grades.

To help reach these targets, the school system is building its own data warehouse to bring all student data together in one place. The ultimate goal is to "democratize" the data so that classroom teachers will be able to easily access it and analyze it themselves to judge the effects of their own school or classroom-based interventions, said Kamalkant Chavda, Boston's assistant superintendent for research, assessment, and evaluation.

FIGURE 3.3   *Boston performance goal: Algebra I in grade 8*

Statement of problem	A majority of students who complete eighth-grade math are not exempt from taking Algebra I in ninth grade.
Performance history	Districtwide, 19% of eighth graders took high school Algebra I in SY 2007–09. (87% of eighth graders took Algebra I in exam schools; 1% of eighth graders took Algebra I in nonexam schools.)
	Of the nonexam school students who took Math 8 in SY 2007–08, 11.5% received a B or better on the final exam, a requirement for placing out of Algebra I in ninth grade.
Performance targets SY 2008–09	28% of Math 8 students will receive a B or better on the final exam.
	Align math curriculum, and train teachers to teach Algebra I in eighth grade.
	Develop criteria for selecting students, and identify supports for them (e.g., step-up summer program).
Performance targets SY 2009–10	45% of Math 8 students will receive a B or better on the final exam.
	10% of nonexam school students will take Algebra I in eighth grade.
Performance targets SY 2010–11	62% of Math 8 students will receive a B or better on the final exam.
	20% of nonexam school students will take Algebra I in eighth grade.
Performance targets SY 2011–12	80% of Math 8 students will receive a B or better on the final exam.
	30% of nonexam school students will take Algebra I in eighth grade.

Source: Boston Public Schools.

The school board, however, will use the annual targets within the goals to monitor progress and to evaluate the superintendent annually, Chavda said. Presentations to the board at regular meetings will also be tied to the acceleration goals, he said. A recent presentation to the board on credit recovery for high schoolers, for example, was related to the district's goal for decreasing the annual dropout rate from 7.9 percent in 2007 to 3 percent or lower by 2012.

DATA FOR EVERY DISTRICT

Thanks to the federal requirement that states and districts track the progress of subgroups and compute the Adequate Yearly Progress of each subgroup, technology is now available to small districts that might not be able to afford to build their own data warehouse, says Katheryn Gemberling. Gemberling is a consultant who works with districts across the country on data use. She is also a coauthor of NSBA's *Key Work* guidebook for boards. At NSBA, she's called the "data diva."

Gemberling has a number of takeaways for boards that want to use data effectively to understand and monitor student achievement in their districts.

To begin with, make sure your district has both leading and lagging indicators to monitor achievement, she said. Because state test results are reported to the district months after students have taken the tests, they are considered *lagging indictors. Leading indicators* are those that teachers and district personnel can use to signal to teachers how well students will do on the tests *before* they take them, when there is still time to inform instruction or to intervene. Districts have a lot of choice about what leading indicator to use, "but if you don't have it in your district, you need to get it," she said.

Next, rather than becoming number crunchers, board members should learn the right questions to ask, said Gemberling. For example, when someone asks how your students are doing, "a bell should go off in your head," she said. Then the members should ask, "Compared to what?" Whether you are looking at test scores, attendance figures, or any other measure, board members need to ask three questions: How did we do compared to the standard (the target)? How did we do compared to ourselves (the trend)? How did we do compared to others (such as comparable districts in the state)? Using all three lenses matters because a decision based only on the answer to the first might be entirely different from one based on the answers to all three.

To demonstrate, Gemberling poses this challenge to board members: Say your district is way above its target on reading, but missed the target on math. If you stop there, you might think more resources and effort should be going into math. After looking at trend data, however, you discover that reading hasn't improved, but math has. However, when compared to the state or your peer districts, your district's results are at the bottom in reading and at the top in math. How can that be? The answer, Gemberling says: low targets have been set for reading. Therefore, a board would most likely come to the opposite conclusion from the initial one, which took only the local targets into account.

She also cautions boards about making decisions based on data about whether an intervention has worked to raise achievement and whether it should be continued. Boards also need to ask about the fidelity of implementation before drawing conclusions. For example, were expectations for how interventions were supposed to be implemented actually met? "There is a tendency to make a policy and look later to see if the results were different. But first you have to be able to answer the question, 'Did we do what we said we were going to do?' Unless you build in evidence gathering that will give you information to what extent it was implemented properly, accurate conclusions from the data can't be drawn," said Gemberling.

Gemberling encourages boards to ask for data reports that are color coded to indicate where students are on standards, or targets, and on progress. In her experience, colors based on the traffic light or the rainbow convey information instantly. "Anchor your target (i.e., proficient) at green. Missed will be red; if kids are close, use yellow." For trend data, green stands for statistically significant improvement; red for statistically significant decline. If there are five levels of measurement versus three, use the colors of the rainbow. "Color helps people get the idea, and then they'll engage. Most people are data phobic, and so they won't engage," she said.

As for how much data boards need, Gemberling uses this rule of thumb: look at what you need to make the decisions you need to make. Typically, boards look at data in depth once or twice a year to make budget decisions, set and monitor goals, and evaluate the superintendent. While many types of assessments are used by educators, board members do not need to see all of them. Privacy issues and efficiency (remember DRIP) come into play. Some school boards and superintendents are creating "data dashboards" to help keep their eye on the big picture of student outcomes in important categories. (See appendix B, "Norfolk Data Dashboard.")

Just as important as deciding which data to monitor is modeling *how* to use data, said Gemberling. Using it as a tool to solve problems is one way; using it to punish and blame is another. "When you get the truth and you don't like the truth, if you turn around and attack the staff, you can be assured the truth won't come to you—I've seen it," she said. "If you look at data as a weapon, it will never work for you; if you use it as information and feedback to guide decisions, it will always work for you."

She also cautions boards that "data alone will not fix the problems." "Weighing myself twelve times a day is not going to cause me to lose weight," she quips. "Having data doesn't guarantee that boards will make good decisions." For example, she recalled the case of a board that refused to eliminate two hundred of two thousand paraprofessional (teacher aide) positions even after the superintendent documented the lack of effectiveness of the policy in the district. "If you do make a political decision that goes against the evidence, then you can't turn around and hold the superintendent and staff accountable for the subsequent results," she said. On the other hand, she said, "Sometimes data can be your friend and help you make a politically unpopular decision, because everyone can see the evidence."

CHAPTER FOUR

Avoiding Pitfalls

Ethics, Norms, and Values   Self-Policing   Problem-Solving

ATLANTA, GA • TUKWILA, WA • BLOOMFIELD, CT

On July 1, 2003, a new law passed by the Georgia state legislature took effect to fundamentally change the operations of the Atlanta school board. In the months and years leading up to this event, it was clear from many in this city of fifty thousand public school students, three-quarters of whom are poor, that the future of quality education in the city had come to a critical crossroads.

Prior to this date, the community had endured years of open conflict between micromanaging board members to the point that one news-paper reporter referred to board meetings as "must-see TV."[1] Student achievement was abysmally low. Five superintendents had come and gone from Atlanta in ten years, and six months after arriving, the new-est superintendent, Beverly Hall, was also threatening to leave.

Hall told associates she was spending up to 40 percent of her time dealing with board members, who were competing with her attempts to manage staff. "The behavior, the culture was such that the administra-tive staff expected direction from the board, they were nervous about offending the board, they felt their jobs depended on whether or not certain members of the board liked them," Hall recalled in a story pub-lished in *Georgia Trend* magazine.[2] One board member felt free to go into schools and "scold" teachers and students. "I could not get principals and staff to focus on my vision because they were getting directions from elsewhere," Hall said.

Community groups banded together with the business community to get legislation passed that would provide checks on the board. One coalition member, the Atlanta Chamber of Commerce, began recruiting and endorsing candidates for the school board through the Edu-PAC political action committee.

The 2003 law remade the Atlanta board in several ways. It reduced the number of board members from fifteen to nine. Members were banned from interfering with the selection of principals. Subcommittees were limited to three directly relating to board responsibilities of budget oversight, accountability, and the superintendent's evaluation. The law doubled the term of the board chair from one year to two and established an ethics commission to hear complaints from any registered voter about any potential violations of a new ethics policy.

Atlanta is an extreme case. But it's a good example of the pitfalls and consequences for boards in the age of accountability. Looking out for yourself, or your own band of constituents, is not job number one and is no longer tolerated.

Atlanta's story is also a powerful one for demonstrating how much students gain when a board understands its role beyond electoral and constituent politics and disciplines itself to operate within that role in collaboration with a knowledgeable superintendent.

In testimony to Congress in 2008, Hall named the coalition's efforts to recruit new members to the Atlanta board and to reform its operations as the number one reason why the "broken" urban system was on its way to being "fixed." Eight years into her work, Hall could report that the percentages of fourth graders meeting or exceeding state standards had climbed from 47 percent to 86 percent; every elementary school had made AYP in 2006–2007, and graduation rates and scores on the National Assessment of Educational Progress (NAEP) tests were climbing. In 2009, Hall was named superintendent of the year by the American Association of School Administrators.

"We have had an opportunity to prove the point that elected boards can work, but you have to have some norms, values, and procedures in place," said the current chair, LaChandra Butler Burks, who supported the charter change and was one of the candidates recruited by the Atlanta chamber.

A number of policy changes—some mandated by the new law as well as others subsequently set up by the board—helped the board and superintendent to focus on teaching, learning, and other needed reforms, according to Butler Burks. The limits on subcommittees, for example, have helped the board focus on its primary responsibilities while freeing up the superintendent and her staff from the demands of preparing for and attending a plethora of meetings. "The staff was spending a lot of time at [sub]committee meetings, and then had to turn around and prepare for the full school board meeting," she said. Expanding the term of the chair has cut down on the amount of internal politicking. "Before, half the year was work; the other half was lobbying," she said. The ethics policy has helped members understand the difference between governance and management, she said.

The board restructured its meetings as well. Once a month, the board meets in a legislative meeting to vote on recommendations and other matters. The week prior to voting, there is a community input meeting, as well as a meeting of the Committee of the Whole to discuss new proposals and receive updates.

The new structure has also allowed the board and superintendent to work in partnership, said Butler Burks. Major reforms to raise student achievement—like the Project GRAD K–12 college readiness initiative, the opening of two single-gender academies, and a $64 million high school reform project to break up Atlanta's large high schools into smaller schools or academies of four hundred over a five-year period—were seriously vetted by the board. Members challenged the superintendent to phase in all systemwide reforms beginning with the city's lowest-performing schools, she said. "There's a lot of research done into the reform initiatives—a lot of presentations, data, and discussion of expected outcomes. We are far from a rubber stamp. The superintendent makes recommendations, but the information has to come. But for the [board] approval of the budget, the reform models would not be in place. You have a board that really takes its fiscal responsibility seriously for the taxpayers that vote you into office, and we want to make sure that we have really tested the waters to make sure it's the best for our children."

The relationship between the board and superintendent is "very good," she added. "The thing I like about it: no one feels they can't question even though we are not educational experts. A lot of times we logically think through the implications of something, and we can challenge her, but in a respectful way. We try to define a process where this can happen."

The school board and the superintendent have also worked together to put a strategic plan in place based on three systemic goals (see figure 4.1). In quarterly retreats, the board monitors progress toward specific targets outlined in the strategic plan using a "balanced scorecard" system. Rather than look at lots of numbers, the board is given a report with a page for each objective. A colored box at the top of the page indicates whether the district is on track to make the annual targets or not: green is "on target," yellow indicates "slow progress," and red is "no progress." If a target is yellow or red, the superintendent must also at the same meeting present a plan for getting to green by the next quarterly meeting, or explain why the objective won't be met.

The board has made its own additions to the balanced scorecard, including items to monitor student attendance (five days of absences triggers an intervention), staff attendance at community meetings, and customer service (phone calls must be returned within three days). (See appendix C, "Atlanta Balanced Scorecard.")

The board has also put in place a variety of other systems to make sure it is modeling the type of collaboration necessary to stay on track with its student achievement goals. In addition to the ethics policy, the Atlanta board worked in two retreats with facilitators from the Pana-

FIGURE 4.1 *Atlanta Public Schools goals*

- Achieve excellence in instruction and education delivery.
- Achieve excellence in facilities and the learning environment.
- Achieve excellence in business operations.

Source: Atlanta Public Schools.

sonic Foundation to create a set of norms and values for its operations and then voted them into policy (see figure 4.2). "The process of creating it has contributed to a sense of teamwork on the board, because it's something that we worked on as a group," said Butler Burks. "We have ownership of the values. I am a believer that because we have different personalities, we aren't always going to agree, but we have some board norms and values. One states, if we don't agree, if a majority supports it, when we walk out of the room, we all support it."

It's not as easy as it sounds, she acknowledges. "Do we really speak with one voice? That is hard. Sometimes I will hear [a dissenting member] say, 'Well, you know, it was a *board* decision.' It's something that we have to constantly remind ourselves about."

To help, Butler Burks pulls out the norms and values document before every meeting. She expects other members to "call her on the carpet if they see me slipping." The Atlanta Public Schools (APS) general counsel is also there to remind them if directives stray into the realm

---

FIGURE 4.2 *Atlanta school board norms of interaction*

- We will speak with one voice.
- We will recognize a single official "voice" of the board.
- We will be clear about, and stay true to, the role of the board.
- We will build trusting relationships.
- We will be on time and prepared for meetings.
- We will respect all persons presenting to the board.
- We will respect staff and fellow board members at all times.
- We will advocate for Atlanta Public Schools and public education. We readily accept our roles as ambassadors for the school system, promoting support for public education and spreading the news of our success.
- We will communicate positively about other board members, staff, and the system.
- We will strive to represent common interests rather than factions. We will make decisions that are best for students in all cases: *all* means *all*.

Source: Atlanta Public Schools.

of the superintendent's side of the operations. Butler Burks, a native of Atlanta who attended Atlanta Public Schools and serves as deputy director of Atlanta's Enterprise Community Partners, a nonprofit affordable housing organization, said she believes members don't intentionally overstep their role, however. "If members struggle with [micromanagement], they struggle with it because of their passion. We get passionate about things."

As chair, she also works hard to forge consensus on the board, aiming for unanimous votes. Split votes can perpetuate divisions in the community, something that is detrimental to ambitious reforms. "When people have a sense that you could have a split vote, [groups] will prey on boards for various things," she explained.

To help build consensus, she tries to makes sure questions and concerns about agenda items are answered before meetings. Board members get the agenda a week in advance and are asked to submit all their questions to the board administrator. They are compiled by Butler Burks and sent to Hall. Members can still ask questions at the meeting, and if something emerges that is controversial for several members, there is an agreement that the item will be "pulled" from the agenda and deferred to the next meeting, which gives members a chance to request more information or suggest changes. If there is something on the agenda that may be potentially controversial among some members, Butler Burks will contact them individually before the meeting. "I think it's important to work people through to a comfort level, or at least a level of understanding," she said.

At the beginning of 2009, the board voted to close three schools and merge the students into several existing schools. (Seventeen schools have been closed during Hall's tenure.) It took two months to work through concerns about closing one of them, she said. After four community meetings and four staff meetings, plans were made for a parade to join the school communities and for team-building exercises for staff. The vote to close the school was unanimous.

Butler Burks acknowledges that this level of collaboration has caused some pushback. "School board meetings used to be like prime time television. Now people don't watch them—they say they are too boring," she said. "People tell me, 'No one asks questions,' 'Nobody votes no!'

(Some votes have been 7–2, she says.) Well, it's because we work so hard by the time it comes for a vote."

"We feel there needs to be some public education about how school boards [should] operate instead of us going back to operating the old way," she added. "We're admitting it's hard, but we also think that if we don't work at it, there would be an impact on sustaining the work of the superintendent as well as the academic achievement. You don't want constant superintendent turnover, because 'the board is crazy,' everybody coming in with new ideas and no stability for the students."

Norms and values statements are becoming more prevalent as school boards both big and small realize the high stakes of failing to put students and education above partisan or constituent politics. In 2008, five years after Atlanta's board charter was changed by the state legislature, the Clayton County school district lost its accreditation due to board mismanagement, sparking another round of legislative proposals, this time aiming to place to restrictions on boards across the state, and granting the state board of education the power to intervene as a last resort. The resulting legislation, Senate Bill 84, failed to pass during the 2009 legislative session, but supporters have vowed to try again.

GET SOME NORMS AND VALUES

Most board members still have to run for office—and often face the perennial question at election time: what have you done for me lately? How they answer this question, how they use their position to educate their constituents about the board's role in increasing student achievement, as well as other educational outcomes, separates the board members of the twenty-first century from those of the past.

In Tukwila, Washington, a small community with 2,700 students outside Seattle, there is no newspaper to cover school board meetings. Board members are often seen out and about. They are magnets for those who want to talk about the local schools. "I can't go out to the grocery store or a soccer game without getting questions," said board president Mary Fertakis. Sometimes the questions are about things that board members aren't supposed to be involved with, like responding to individual complaints about teachers or staff.

While it's a board member's job to listen, an individual member has no authority to solve problems unilaterally. Without a prearranged agreement on how to handle these situations, a well-meaning school board member can easily get derailed.

A former Peace Corps volunteer, Fertakis was a representative member of the Washington State Business Roundtable, a coalition of the thirty-five largest corporations in the state, when the state legislature passed its education reform law. She had an infant at the time, but it was clear to her that "reform would take a long time," so she decided it was not too early to get involved. She wrote to the Tukwila superintendent asking if there was anything she could do to help. Suddenly, she became cochair of the local Essential Learning Goals Task Force. She applied for a vacant spot on the school board but was not appointed by the board. When the next election year rolled around, she ran for the spot and got elected. Fertakis said she was motivated to help with some big-picture things that needed doing in the district. There was no strategic plan to meet the state's new standards, to form partnerships with the community, or to objectively evaluate the superintendent, she says. And there was a problem with trust on the board; information from the board's confidential executive sessions, which are used in rare occasions to prepare for negotiations or to deal with personnel matters, appeared to be leaking out. One member made it clear to the others that she saw her role as protecting the interests of teaching staff.

Together, the Tukwila board developed a set of operating principles that has served it well in many dicey situations, said Fertakis. (See figure 4.3.) One important norm is called "following the chain of command"; another is "no surprises." Fertakis uses both routinely. For example, not long ago, a teacher called her with some specific complaints. Fertakis stopped her before she continued. "I told her that I would listen, but that anything she was telling me, I would be telling the superintendent, and if she was comfortable with that, I would be happy to talk to her." Then, Fertakis followed up with phone calls or e-mails about the situation to her colleagues and the superintendent so they would be in the loop. "It's working for us, but every time we bring on a new board member, we go over those protocols one by one. There can be a boo-boo at times, but nothing intentional. We have them in writing and publish them for all those who come to meetings," she said.

FIGURE 4.3   *Tukwila, Washington, norms*

Tukwila School District Board of Directors Operating Principles

For the purpose of enhancing teamwork among members of the board, and between the members and the administration, we, the members of the Tukwila School District board of directors, do hereby publicly commit ourselves collectively and individually to the following operating principles.

The board of directors will:

1. Represent the needs and interests of all students in the district.

2. Exercise leadership in vision, planning, policy making, evaluation, and advocacy on behalf of the students and district, not in managing the day-to-day operations of the district.

3. Provide continuing education opportunities and support to each other.

4. Conduct its business through a set agenda. Emerging items will be addressed in subsequent meetings through agenda items.

5. Provide full disclosure. Each member will provide input, encouragement, express concerns and positions rather than withhold information from other members. When a board member feels that there has not been full disclosure, an objective process for revisiting the issue will be used.

6. Maintain an open environment where each member is empowered to freely express opinions, concerns, and ideas. Board members will work together to clarify and restate discussions in order to strive for full understanding.

7. Keep an open mind and accept that they can change their opinions by recognizing that they are not locked into their initial stated positions.

8. Make decisions on information and not on personalities. Board members will act with the best information available at the time considering data, the superintendent's recommendations, proposals, and suggestions. Board members will strive to make the best decisions at the time, without waiting for the perfect decision.

9. Debate the issues, not one another. The board will engage in critical thinking, expecting all board members to freely offer differing points of view as part of the discussion, prior to making a board decision.

10. Not take unilateral action. A board member's authority is derived through the majority of the board acting as a whole during an open public meeting.

11. Attend meetings well prepared to discuss issues on the agenda, and will be prepared to make decisions, striving for efficient decision making.

(continued)

FIGURE 4.3 *(continued)*

12. Strive to have no surprises for the board or superintendent. Surprises will be the exception. All members will receive the same information in a timely manner.

13. Reach decisions by consensus, and individual members will publicly abide by those decisions.

14. Follow the chain of command and direct others to do the same. Personnel complaints and concerns will be directed to the superintendent.

15. Review and revise operating principles, as needed, as part of the board's self-evaluation.

Source: Tukwila School District.

In addition, the board also meets monthly at 7 a.m. on Saturdays to have breakfast with the superintendent. "This gives us an opportunity to discuss issues of interest or concern and hear what each other thinks," said Fertakis. "Everyone feels heard, and we've created an environment where all members can say what they think," she said.

The operating protocols have been key to getting on track. The district is now on its third strategic plan focused on achievement, and has documented significant progress for students who have remained in the district from fourth through tenth grade.

SELF-POLICE

High-functioning boards don't just define roles and ways of operating, they police them.

New members, in particular, need guidance. They may not know, for example, that it's important to continue to sign in to schools as visitors, because as individual school board members, they have no special rights. They may also need help in dealing with difficult personnel situations where the law forbids them from explaining why a popular teacher (or superintendent) has been dismissed, despite ardent pleas for explanations from their neighbors.

Oftentimes, a chair will speak to a member privately if they have done something that appears to go against the norms. In other cases, the whole board works to make sure that members don't "slip," to use Butler Burks's phrase. "If someone gets off on a tangent, we have to reel them back in," said Leni Patterson of the Laurens District 55, South Carolina, board.

In Berlin, Connecticut, the board goes so far as to ask administrators to anonymously evaluate the performance of the school board as a check. "If we are saying we are part of this process, we need to hear how we are doing," said Gary Brochu, the chair. Through the annual evaluations, the board learned there was "sensitivity about turf" among the staff, he said. "It's something that we keep in mind. If someone points out that we are stepping over, and if members disagree, it's an opportunity to have a conversation" about roles and boundaries, Brochu said. (See appendix D, "Berlin Board of Education Self-Evaluation.)

Micromanaging staff is a "pervasive problem among school districts, even those in which the board is strongly committed to ensuring executive accountability," the Panasonic Foundation concluded in its board report.[3] The foundation recommends that boards be very explicit about defining roles of the board and the superintendent, recommending even that boards refer to the superintendent as the "chief executive" in order to make more clear the superintendent's role in running the school district and overseeing the evaluation of the rest of the district staff. It advises boards to use preestablished criteria for evaluating the superintendent and to insist that members stay out of staff-level decisions. "Even well-intentioned intrusions by the board into staff decisions [send] the signal to staff that the board is also the chief executive." Role confusion can undercut the board's ability to hold the superintendent accountable and tie the district and board in knots. The Panasonic Foundation advises all boards to adopt a code of conduct, which it includes in a handy summary of board best practices called board "rights and wrongs." (See figure 4.4.) "The problem for boards isn't having conflict among members' views and opinions," write the authors of Panasonic's board guide, "it is how to manage the conflict so that the 'exchange' of ideas is productive and leads to good board policies and actions."[4] Boards should lay out the rules for dialogue and decision making, and keep in mind that once the board makes a decision, individual members must abide by it since individuals have no authority on their own, the authors write.

FIGURE 4.4 *Board rights and wrongs*

"Rights"	"Wrongs"
Act on behalf of all citizens, including future generations impacted by the board's actions.	Act on behalf of only those citizens who supported individual members in their election campaign or who talk regularly with individual members.
Act as a board in setting vision, values, and objectives. Find common ground.	Avoid the difficult conversations. Let differences in personal viewpoints keep the board perpetually divided.
Fulfill the four duties of a board.	Attend to the staff's job; "second guess" what the staff should/should not do.
Establish a board plan around how it will use its areas of authority to achieve the district's vision, values, and expected results. Be accountable for creating the conditions necessary to achieve expected results.	Avoid making a commitment to a planned course of action; let the board's actions be driven by decisions made at meetings based on issues brought by staff. Blame the superintendent/staff if results are not met.
State those areas in which the superintendent must get board approval before acting, and keep the "see us first" areas to a minimum.	Attempt to direct staff actions by having the superintendent run everything by the board.
Establish a code of conduct with processes and consequences for holding members accountable to it.	Avoid taking a stance on acceptable and unacceptable board member behavior and articulating this in writing.

Source: Patricia Mitchell, Andrew Gelber, Sophie Sa, and Scott Thompson, "Doing the Right Thing: The Panasonic Foundation's Guide for Effective School Boards" (draft, the Panasonic Foundation, Secaucus, NJ, 2009).

BLOCKING AND TACKLING

Even after adopting norms and values and attempting to self-police, boards struggle with members who just don't get it. These members continue to operate outside the board norms or agreed-upon principles even after board presidents and other members have reminded them or even publicly called them to task. This is one of the most difficult problems for school boards to deal with. After all, members have the right to free speech, and, most often, they were put on the board by the will of the voters.

It's not uncommon to find that it only takes one or two members who decide to champion a constituent interest or a single issue apart from the district's overall goals to disrupt the work of a board. These individuals are the ones who, for example, go into schools and tell principals what to do and attempt to undercut the superintendent's authority. They are not "team players." They misunderstand that although they may be elected through a democratic process, they are not empowered as an individual to act. In the world of school boards, there is a name for such individuals—outliers—and it's not a compliment.

Tom Gentzel has been working with school boards in Pennsylvania for twenty-nine years. He has another name for renegade board members: "the nickel in the dryer."

"The concept is about getting attention for the wrong reasons," explained Gentzel, the executive director of the Pennsylvania School Boards Association (PSBA). "What happens on some of these boards is that there are one or two who are members behaving badly. They don't just make noise, but really impact the board. If it's one or two people, it [can] solidify the board to make sure they are isolated because they only have one vote. In some cases it can almost be a good thing, because it can strengthen the resolve of the others. But it can also bring the whole board functioning to a halt by sowing distrust." (Board members who follow the rules and refrain from pushing single issues are penalized—or seen as too passive by constituents—if others are allowed to pursue their own agendas, for example.)

"It doesn't always translate into the district not doing well by kids. Other members can make the best of things, but it's extraordinarily hard," said Gentzel. "Fortunately, nickels tend to wash though the system. They don't last very long. But they can create public relations problems for the district."

Gentzel believes dysfunctional boards are the exception. However, while most boards do a good job, they can go through some "rough patches," he said. To help its member districts, PSBA has published a set of governance standards with benchmark questions boards can use to talk about how well they are operating within them. Eighty percent of its five hundred member boards have adopted the PSBA's code of conduct that incorporates its governance standards (see box 4.1). "We're really trying to transform ourselves into a professional society of school boards. Even though it's voluntary service, it's incredibly important: if a board isn't doing its own job right, the school system will be hampered," Gentzel said.

Maintaining up-to-date policies and having a clear process for building meeting agendas are two ways boards can deal with disruptive members, he said. If boards have a "policy on new policies" (see figure 4.5), for example, they can more easily deflect an outlier who may try

---

BOX 4.1

PSBA Code of Conduct for Members of Pennsylvania School Boards

Preamble
We, as members of our local board of education, representing all the residents of our school district, believe that:

- Striving toward ideal conditions for effective school board service to our community, in a spirit of teamwork and devotion to public education, is the greatest instrument for preserving and perpetuating our representative democracy.

- The future welfare of this community, commonwealth, and nation depends upon the quality of education we provide in the public schools.

- In order to maintain a free and strong country, our civic obligation to the community, commonwealth, and nation is to maintain free and strong public schools in the United States of America, without surrendering our responsibilities to any other person, group, or organization.

- Boards of school directors share responsibility for ensuring a "thorough and efficient system of public education" as required by the Pennsylvania Constitution.

- Our fellow residents have entrusted us with the advocacy for and stewardship of the education of the youth of this community.

- The public expects that our first and greatest priority is to provide equitable educational opportunities for all youth.

to impose their will on the group by hijacking the meetings with surprise proposals or other tactics because the chair or other members can simply steer them to the appropriate process for changing or adding district policies, said Gentzel. "The board can say, 'That's an interesting thought, but that would require changing policy 23, and there's a process to change policy'—it's a way to channel the let's-do-it-now-I-want-

---

Accordingly,

- The community should be provided with information about its schools and be engaged by the board and staff to encourage input and support for the school system. Devoting time, thought, and study to our duties and responsibilities as school board members is critical for rendering effective and credible service.

- Board members should work together in a spirit of harmony, respect, and cooperation, despite differences of opinion.

- Personal decisions should be based upon all sufficient facts, we should vote our honest conviction without partisan bias, and we will abide by and uphold the majority decision of the board.

- Individuals have no legal authority outside the meetings of the board, and should conduct their relationships with all stakeholders and media on this basis.

- We will not use our positions as school directors to benefit ourselves or any individual or agency.

- School boards must balance their responsibility to provide educational programs with the need to be effective stewards of public resources.

- We should recognize that the primary responsibility of the board is to adopt policies by which the schools are to be administered.

- We should respect that the superintendent of schools and his or her staff are responsible and accountable for the delivery of the educational programs and the conduct of school operations.

- Communication with all stakeholders and the media should be conducted in accordance with board policy.

FIGURE 4.5 *Sample policy on new policies*

SC 301, 407, 510, 511
Pol. 000

The board shall exercise leadership through its rule-making power by adopting board procedures and policies for the organization and operation of the school district. Those procedures and policies which are not dictated by the statutes, or regulations of the state board, or ordered by a court of competent authority may be adopted, amended, or repealed at any meeting of the board, { } provided the proposed adoption, amendment, or repeal has been proposed at a previous board meeting and has remained on the agenda of each succeeding board meeting until approved or rejected.

SC 407

Changes in a proposed board procedure or policy, except for minor editorial revisions, at the second reading shall cause that reading to constitute a first reading.

Source: Pennsylvania School Boards Association.

it-done into a process that's neutral and not aimed at the individual board member. You can just say, 'That's how we handle these things.'"

Board policy about meetings is also important, said Gentzel. How is the agenda constructed? What is required to change it? Board meetings are not "unfettered democracies": while boards have to be careful not to stifle the views of the minority, an individual does not have the right to dominate the meeting, he said. "We really talk to districts about spending time on those basic things," he said. "The blocking and tackling is the football. It's not a magic bullet, but it does say, when you have those renegade board members, there is a way to corral that. If someone just comes in and pushes their weight around, others can say, that's not the way we do it."

DON'T BLAME; SOLVE PROBLEMS

When David Title was in the running to head up the Bloomfield, Connecticut, schools in 2002, he knew what he was getting into. The board had a history of micromanaging, had fired a superintendent, and had gone through two interim superintendents in fifteen months. "This was one of those jobs that no one wanted to touch because they didn't want to deal with the board," he recalled.

He was persuaded to give it a shot, however. Four of the seven board seats had turned over. The board members told Title that they "really wanted to fix the district."

When Title became superintendent in March 2002, the schools had outdated texts, "ancient" curriculum guides that did not align with standards, large class sizes, and persistently low achievement. Of the 2,200 students enrolled in the public schools, 90 percent were African Americans, and less than 50 percent of the students were scoring proficient or above on state tests in some grade levels. "The district I inherited was one of the most dysfunctional districts in the state in almost every way a school district can be," Title recalled. "A lot of the early work was stabilizing the patient, getting it to function as a professionally run school system, and then digging into the student achievement pieces and longer-term planning."

True to its word, the board empowered Title to make many decisions, ceding hiring decisions completely over to him. "One of the first things we did was to define roles for board members and for administrators," said board chair James Michel, audit director at Aetna Inc., who was elected to the board shortly before Title was hired. "We all sat down and had a caucus, and we all agreed that staffing issues are not our role. We have a superintendent to do that. You cannot have seven people on a board deciding who should get fired and who should get hired. That's very inefficient."

In annual retreats with a facilitator from CABE, the board members set out roles, agreed on ways of operating, and changed their meeting schedule, their subcommittees, and their budget approval procedure. Specifically, board members agreed to follow the chain of command, referring parent and constituent calls about problems to Title and his staff. Meetings, which had been long and inefficient in the past, were cut from two per month to one and shortened to only thirty to forty-five minutes in length. Members stick to only those matters on the agenda, with a two-thirds vote of the board required to add items to the agenda during the meeting. Budget meetings became budget workshops where the superintendent briefed board members in detail about academic plans to lower class size, add a new high school program, purchase state-of-the-art technology, and add before- and after-school programs and an early-childhood center. They agreed to compare the performance of their own students' progress against that of previous years and to reach 100 percent proficiency on state tests by 2011, as part of a five-year strategic plan. The percentage of students below basic declined steadily, while the percentage of students scoring proficient and above increased.

"One thing David has done that is critical is to educate the board on what it takes to have a good school system: good instruction, up-to-date curriculum, small class sizes," said Michel, who usually starts his day by phoning Title to check on any developing problems as he drives to work. "We didn't always get good explanations about why these things are important. Now it's easy to buy into. It's helped build our trust in David."

All the groundwork came in handy in 2007 when the tenth-grade test scores "fell apart," and a story about them appeared on the front page of the *Hartford Courant*, according to Michel. Members of the public came to their meeting to protest. While reiterating the general trend upward in scores in the district, Title expressed his disappointment and promised to do a complete analysis of the causes and factors for the results and release the results to the public. The board supported the superintendent, expressing confidence that he would come forward with a plan. "I think when people saw how personal David took it, his attitude kept everyone focused on problems instead of blaming anybody," said Michel. "In business when you have a bad year . . . there's so many things beyond your control. The true sign of a strong leader is, what are you going to do about it?" After a month, Title came up with a strategy for helping struggling high schoolers through tutoring and through a new partnership with a local university.

When Title took the job, outsiders told him that sooner or later, the board would "show its fangs" and interfere with his ability to do his job. That has not come to pass, Title said. "We're in the third year of a five-year plan completely focused on student achievement," he said in late 2008. "We have followed through with what we say we're going to do, and the board likes what has come out of this governance model, so we keep doing it."

CHAPTER FIVE

When Things Go Right

Learning Monitoring Communicating

ELK MOUND, WI • GALLATIN COUNTY, KY •
NORFOLK, VA • WHITE BEAR LAKE, MN

Only about 10 percent of voters cast ballots in local school board elections. Some hold this low turnout as evidence that boards have become irrelevant and have failed to adequately engage, and thus have failed to represent, their community in their schools, their power eclipsed by more powerful teacher unions.[1] However, in the 1960s, on the basis of an ethnographic study of a school board member in the Robertsdale School District, two professors, Frank W. Lutz and Laurence Iannaccone, proposed a different theory that offers a different explanation for low turnouts in school board elections and what they mean for the community, board members, and students.

Lutz and Iannaccone theorized that low turnout and minimal turnover of members on a school board actually means that most community members are satisfied with the way things are going and with the board members who represent them. Large turnout in school board elections is the real sign of trouble, and superintendent and board members need to keep their fingers on the pulse of the community to watch out for growing discontent. Their "Dissatisfaction Theory of American Democracy" posited that democratic school board elections are important because they regularly offer the *opportunity* to bring about needed changes. When enough people feel "things" aren't working, they will go to the polls and pitch out those they feel are responsible. After enough school board seats turn over, typically, the superintendent is next in line to go. Through elections, "citizens can change local education policy and obtain the level of education they choose and are willing to support," wrote Lutz and Iannaccone.[2]

Survey data supports this theory. Curiously, while most Americans say they are dissatisfied with public education in general, a healthy majority are happy with their own local schools.[3] Low turnout for local school board elections may actually mean that most are satisfied with their local school boards, rather than the more commonly heard interpretation: that school boards are irrelevant.

Of course, satisfaction by the public is affected by the quality of the information the public has about its schools. One well-acknowledged benefit of the No Child Left Behind Act is that more complete information is now available about how all students are doing. Schools are no longer able to publish average test scores as proof of how well they are educating children. Under NCLB, districts and schools are responsible for reporting results of state tests by subgroups, which has revealed persistent gaps between white and black and Latino students, abled and disabled, and the poor and nonpoor. It has also given boards some ammunition to fight what some board members call "the real enemy"—the status quo.

On the ground, though, the general state of satisfaction with local schools means that serving on a school board when "things" are going right can be a lonely business. Board members agree that an absence of public comment during meetings—or a dearth of e-mails or phone calls between meetings—is generally a sign of satisfaction, or at least the lack of mass dissatisfaction. High-functioning school boards, however, don't use this as an excuse to slack off. In between periodic goal-setting sessions and evaluations of the superintendent comes the really hard part: professional development to keep up with effective ways of governing; monitoring the affairs of the district at a level that is appropriate for a board; and communicating with and engaging the community in the work of school improvement in order to create a sense of urgency and the support necessary to make educational changes that may be needed.

LEARNING BOARDS

Under the overseer model of the last century, desirable board members—generally those from the worlds of universities and business—were assumed to have the knowledge needed to lead the district based on their position in life and contacts in the community. To be leaders in this century, however, high-functioning school boards train themselves continually. Whether it is through in-house workshops led by administrators, attendance at the national and/or state school board association workshops and annual conventions, online courses on board association Web sites, or in-depth relationships with consultants or facilitators, these boards see learning as essential to doing their job well.

The growing importance of school board training is also being acknowledged by state governments. Twenty states now mandate training for new and/or veteran members, which is usually provided by the state board association.[4]

On the most basic level, members have to keep up with continually changing state and federal mandates and laws, something that district staffers generally help with. They also need to keep up with promising initiatives to raise student achievement in and outside their district as well as continually evolving systems for monitoring data and engaging the community in school improvement. New board members especially need training in their roles and responsibilities and in laws pertaining to ethics and conflicts of interest. The most advanced boards work on operating protocols, handbooks documenting their operations, and board self-evaluations.

One of the districts participating in the Lighthouse Project phase 3 training is in Elk Mound, Wisconsin, a small but growing rural community with 1,100 students located 10 miles west of Eau Claire. Tim Sivertson, a home care and hospice registered nurse, got interested in board development when he became board president in 1999. "I wondered, how *do* you get a board wanting to improve?" he asked.

With help from the Wisconsin school board association, the board members began with an annual self-evaluation and goal-setting meeting, adding a second annual meeting to monitor progress toward the goals midway through the year. They also worked on instituting board norms or protocols, including a "ladder of responsibility," so that board members would refer parents and others to teachers, principals, and the superintendent for questions about personnel and other nonpolicy issues. "We actually do that now," Sivertson said.

To build a sense of teamwork, members agreed to support the majority decisions of the board following any split vote. Communications between any individual board member and the superintendent go out to all members. The board produced a binder of board roles and responsibilities that the district gives to anyone who is considering running for school board. "Right away, off the bat, I want to make sure that we are raising expectations so that potential board members aren't pursuing a single issue," he said. "We've had board members running who have promised a lot of little things to people once they were elected, and I've said, 'Here is some of the information that we have on that . . .' It's not really our role to say we're going to get new basketball uniforms. That just gives the public the perception that the school board is just a good ol' boys club."

The Elk Mound board has worked closely with and has a high level of trust in its superintendent, who was recruited from within, having served as the middle school and high school principal. It has benefited from stability on the board as well. In 2009, all but one member had served for more than twelve years.

In 2006, the Elk Mound board volunteered to be one of the six Wisconsin districts working with the Wisconsin Association of School Boards to pilot test the Lighthouse training in the conditions of school renewal. A data specialist assisted the board with analysis of results on state and local benchmark tests and other data. This has helped them understand and ask critical questions about apparent gaps in learning. It has also helped them make decisions about budget allocations, said Sivertson. "Typically, at board meetings, the guidance counselor came to discuss the test results, but we never went too deep into it. Now we know where the gaps are, and discuss what we need to improve. We look at the overall picture and say, how are you going to improve this? We see this deficiency here; how are you going to raise this? We as a board look at the 40,000-foot view, initiate policy, and then it is up to the administration to look in much more detail and bring the data to us. The integrity of that process gives me the assurance, as a board member, that we are working hard as a district to address achievement. Ultimately, it's our responsibility to put the policy in place that drives improvement." As a result of its work with data, the board realized that there was a need for a reading teacher at the high school.

Through the Lighthouse training, board members learned that "moving" boards with higher levels of achievement also demonstrate the belief that all children can learn at higher levels. So in 2008, when administrators recommended a new goal that all students reach 80 percent proficiency on the state test by 2012, Sivertson made a motion that the district shoot for 100 percent instead. It passed. The high school principal came up later and thanked the board for increasing expectations for student achievement. Also that year, Elk Mound won NSBA's top award, the Magna Award, for its board development.

Board members also have learned strategies for enhancing their outreach efforts to the community. Two members are available to talk informally with members of the public thirty minutes before regular meetings begin. A (nonvoting) student representative was added to the board to represent the student viewpoint. A board newsletter is mailed to every household in the district each month and posted on the school district Web site. A pamphlet with the district vision, core values, and six goals— with action steps devised by the administration for reaching the goals— is also distributed. The superintendent has framed and posted each year's pamphlet for display in the school board meeting room.

The training has changed Sivertson's view of the job, he said.

As board members, sometimes we start to think we know a lot and we know best. Sometimes it's our fault that we don't get out information; sometimes it's the public's for not listening. But the reality is, 70 percent of our district doesn't have anything to do with the schools, but they are taxpayers, too. We have to show how we are improving student success for the economy of Wisconsin and especially [for our students] in a global society. We need public input because we can't do it without them. The public gives us ideas on how we can improve and tells us where we need to do a better job. We have to listen to this, and balance the public input against our legal responsibility to provide a free and appropriate public education to the kids and meet the standards.

Support from the public is also critical for building confidence in the school system, which translates into financial support for public schools, he said. "We've run four referendums; that's how we have to increase our levy to build and meet our financial obligations. There have been times when we do have to be focused on doing a better job informing the public about why we need these funds."

All of this groundwork proved valuable in 2009 when district leaders realized that growing enrollments and aging facilities meant all three of the district's schools had become inadequate. In preparation for a new referendum, the board commissioned a poll of the community on several options. Results showed that most preferred to renovate and expand the existing schools rather than build a new one. But the poll also revealed some other things: most community members said they got most of their news about the schools from the board newsletter; also, most of those polled said they were satisfied with the schools. On April 7, 2009, at a time when job losses around the country were making headlines, the $9.3 million referendum passed 648 to 413. Referendums in four other neighboring districts held on the same day were voted down.

Sivertson hears from boards across Wisconsin with $20 million to $24 million budgets that have minimal or no money budgeted for training, and it frustrates him. "If you were a business, it would be [seen as] an essential part of being effective in improving your outcomes," he said.

Back at NSBA headquarters in Alexandria, Virginia, Joe Villani acknowledges that it can be difficult politically for board members to set aside funds for travel and training for themselves, especially in financially difficult times when they feel pressure to cut their own board budget in solidarity with other departments. NSBA sponsors an annual conference that attracts 5,600 members from across the United States. Many come to participate in the NSBA "boot camp" for new board members during the first day of the conference.

Boards that cut their training budgets are "cutting their own seed corn," he said. "I think professional development for school boards is as important as professional development for surgeons—they need to be kept up to date on successful practices. How can they do things more efficiently and effectively? I think it is very unfortunate that some folks get elected and think they have everything they need to know. Really they are just beginning. It's like when I got my driver's license, I said to my father, 'Now I can drive!' And he said, 'No, now you can *learn* to drive.'"

Given the current accountability requirements, board members need more skills than before, says Villani. Board members need to have enough awareness about educational issues to begin to ask critical questions, and they need enough knowledge about those issues to evaluate the answers, he said. "They need enough experience to begin to formulate policy to institutionalize the answers," he added. "That's the progression I see: awareness, experience, and knowledge, and then you need some real experience with the issues to draft policy."

Training is also important for board members to become "acculturated" to the role, Villani said. "Becoming a better board member means not just picking up the technical skills about how to ask questions about a program, but the subtleties of how to promote a good culture and climate," he said. "Learning about how to handle the issues and instances that come at you as a school board member can't be learned in isolation, but by mingling with more experienced members from your district and others."

What kind of skills does it take to be a good board member? I asked him. "Some ability to analyze data, or know what it can provide," said Villani. "They need to be critical thinkers and have a vision that student achievement is possible for every student, and that sometimes that means a variety of applications—not a one-size-fits-all approach. It's very hard work, and you have to think against and act against the status quo. That's your worst enemy." Board members need to understand the value of the school in a community, and they need to be in it for students, "not for themselves," he said, adding, "One of the big threats to school board governance is the single-issue candidate."

In the age of accountability, boards today need help moving from the "small picture" concerns of boards of yesteryear (think hiring the football coach) to the "big picture" concerns of today, says Villani. Training available in state associations is also evolving to help boards make the shift.

The Maryland Association of Boards of Education (MABE), whose membership is made up of all twenty-four boards in the entire state, now has five levels of training for board members. Beginners start with a one-and-a-half-day "bootstrap" orientation to the nuts and bolts of serving. The Academy and Leadership 1 and Leadership 2 courses give board members a chance to take specialized classes in negotiations or budgeting, to observe other board members, or to do a project like a handbook about their board's operating procedures. The master board program involves a yearlong "self-study" by a board.

"Having a progression of classes helps new board members get a better handle on what boards are about," said Kitty Blumsack, MABE's director of board development. "The expectation is that if you want kids to learn, you should be a master learner." Boards that train themselves also model the importance of professional development to school staff, she said, and send the message, "If the board is learning, we should be learning," she said.

Seventeen-year veteran board member Rebecca Burgett of the Gallatin County (Kentucky) Board of Education credits training that her board received for helping to change the culture of the board and the district to elevate the importance of education to the future of the children in her rural area. "I put a lot of stock in training," said Burgett. "We've definitely evolved."

With 4 schools and an enrollment of 1,600, the district is located in farm country between Louisville and Cincinnati. Most adults have to drive out of the area for work. The percentage of poor students has climbed from 50 percent to more than 60 percent since she's been on the board, and so has the number of Hispanic English language learners. A former PTA mom, Burgett has stayed on the board even though her two sons are now grown. "It didn't take me long to find out that there are some kids where nobody's fighting for them. It's just something I believe in. All kids need someone to advocate for them; I knew my kids would be fine."

Through the state board association's ASAP (Advancing Student Achievement to Proficiency) program, the board began by analyzing its agenda. "We asked ourselves, are we spending time on student achievement or brick-and-mortar issues?" The board decided it was the latter, so facilities and other routine matters that the board had to sign off on were put in a single consent agenda that could be passed with one motion. "We can always pull something off and talk about it if there's a concern; we want to focus our time on the really important things." Now every meeting features some kind of presentation about students or staff to highlight student achievement.

The board also became very data oriented, said Burgett.

> For many years, in our early years, we were involved in sports. Everyone was excited by the volleyball team—just the wrong things. Now we look at our budget. We look at our budget; we look at our state tests scores, ACT scores, Explore results (a college readiness test for seventh and eighth graders), and curriculum alignment. We ask what's working, what's not working. It's really an ongoing process. With Kentucky's budgeting process, you have to project what your budget is going to be, and you are always adjusting based on attendance. It is the system we have to work with. So it's continual. We are always asking, where are we, where are we going to go?

In 2002, the board hired Dot Perkins as superintendent. A former student in the district and championship basketball coach, Perkins had been a teacher and administrator since 1981. "She has a vested interest in the district and works day and night—she's awesome," said Burgett. "She's really challenged us to go to the next level by thinking outside the box. She has high expectations for staff. When she talks, we listen—it's a mutual respect." On every board agenda and communication from the superintendent's office is the same motto: "What's Best for Kids."

Under Perkins's leadership, the district also volunteered to undergo the Kentucky voluntary assistance process along with Madison County. It has made a priority of offering full-day kindergarten even though it does not get fully reimbursed by the state. Teachers, with Perkins's blessing, lobbied the board to invest in a new literacy program, which was also a big expense, given the district's $8 million budget. Both initiatives have proved to be well worth it in terms of student results, and dropout rates have fallen dramatically. Perkins invites board members to regular focus groups with students and senior citizens and to "Monitoring Mondays," when she and her staff visits schools to look for evidence of improvements.

Most visitors to the board meetings, however, come to talk about personnel issues, said Burgett. This is despite the fact that the 1990 Kentucky education reform law gave the power to hire and fire personnel to superintendents, principals, and school-based councils. Perkins agrees that the pressure on board members to get involved in hiring for jobs and other minutiae can be intense. "We all grew up here. We all know everybody. It is awkward sometimes," she said. However, the board is very well trained and doesn't micromanage, she said. If a hiring or other administrative matter comes up from a constituent, board members will "look them in the eye and say, 'I cannot discuss this at this time; talk to Dot.'"

Training that the board members have received has helped in learning about boundaries such as these, Burgett said.

> When you get on the board, it's overwhelming. You come on with thoughts of what you are going to do when you get on the board. But the first thing you learn is what you can do and what you can't do, and here's the law, and this is what happens if you do. There's always the micromanager, the person who wants to run the school or wants to go into the lunchroom and tell them to stop doing something, and as a board member, it just has no place. As parents, we've all had issues with a teacher, but it's important to drop it at the board level and not publicly embarrass or say negative things about staff, because it's inappropriate and unprofessional. Maybe our intentions are good, but the perceptions are bad, and we need to be aware of that.

As other high-functioning boards do, the Gallatin County board works hard to appear united in public. "If I see there is majority to support something, I want to support that decision," said Burgett. "I have seen so many boards that don't do that."

As a trainer with the Kentucky School Boards Association, Burgett has witnessed shockingly bad board behavior in other districts, including public fights over committee chairmanships and personal attacks. "I try to explain to people how that comes across. It doesn't come off as support, and the audience and the newspapers say, what the heck, these people can't agree. So the board doesn't have respect, the newspapers are putting the controversies on the front page, and the staff is saying, I don't know if I want to be here. I come back loving my board.

We have disagreements, but we keep it professional, and when it's over, it's over," she said.

MONITORING AND ALIGNING

In addition to the annual or semiannual retreats with the superintendents to review progress toward the goals (or strategic plan), high-functioning boards are adopting a variety of strategies to monitor the work of the district, as well as their own progress as a governing body, throughout the year.

Monitoring the work of the leadership of the district and whether it makes a difference for students is one strategy that NSBA calls "alignment." To explain this concept, Villani recalls a remark that a colleague made when he was serving on the board of Montgomery County, Maryland: "He asked, 'Are all of these knobs that we are turning connected to anything?'" The most sophisticated boards also monitor themselves by self-evaluations or self-assessments (see figure 5.1).

One common strategy to help a board monitor the work of the district is for the chair, in consultation with the rest of the board, to schedule presentations on those things that the board is most concerned about following when it comes to the district's goals or targets, as done in Boston and Atlanta. Boards that use policy governance get regular monitoring reports from the superintendent. In Norfolk, Virginia, the board even developed a format for staff to use in making five- to fifteen-minute presentations, in order to make sure that the board would keep the focus on what it needed to know about, rather than get bogged down in the educational or administrative details (see figure 5.2).

COMMUNICATING/ENGAGING THE PUBLIC

While professional educators are in charge of the day-to-day operations of schools, board members are uniquely positioned to advocate on behalf of the needs of the school district. As elected or appointed representatives, board members have the ties to the community and the credibility needed to sell the public on important changes in schools as

FIGURE 5.1 *NSBA's board self-assessment*

Rate your board using four categories—fully achieved, mostly achieved, partially achieved, and beginning to achieve—for each of the statements below:

1. We have established a specific and limited set of priorities for improving student achievement that gives everyone in the district clear focus.

2. We make staffing and resource allocation decisions based on our student achievement priorities.

3. We ensure resource equity for schools by providing additional supports to schools in communities with higher needs.

4. We view the budget as the vehicle for accomplishing our priorities rather than simply as our spending plan.

5. We leverage resources within our budget to achieve our priorities.

6. We add or delete programs and initiatives based on analysis of data and district priorities.

7. We have no sacred cows in our budget.

8. Our curriculum and program initiatives are directly aligned to our student achievement priorities.

9. Our textbook, instructional materials, and technology selections are directed by our student achievement priorities.

10. Our staff training is designed exclusively to support our student achievement priorities.

11. All units in the district, including all support services, focus on their role in accomplishing the student achievement priorities.

12. As a board, the criteria we use to make all decisions are our student achievement priorities.

Source: Used with permission from *The Key Work of School Boards: A Guidebook.* © 2009 by the National School Boards Association. All rights reserved.

well as the need to raise funds for initiatives related to student achievement, like class-size reductions, new curriculum, or facility upgrades. Conversely, in a downturn, the board may need to use its ties to solicit help in establishing priorities. (For an example of how boards can evaluate their communication and engagement capabilities, see box 5.1, "Benchmarks and Questions for Communication and Engagement.")

FIGURE 5.2   *Norfolk's format for staff reports to the board*

1. **Define the issue or question.** What is the key question we are seeking answers for? What is the core problem we are trying to solve? How does it relate to our four targets or performance measures?

2. **Provide brief overview/background information.** What are our current practices in this area? What is working? What are the challenges? Are there deadlines involved?

3. **Provide recommendations.** What must change? What alternatives are there? Can we engage in a partnership to help solve the problem or achieve a goal?

4. **Provide budget implications.** How much will this change cost or save? How can we demonstrate that this action is an effective use of resources?

5. **Provide a statement of impact.** How will this action improve student achievement/student behavior? How will it impact our climate/culture? How will it help us "move the needle" toward becoming world-class?

6. **Identify potential policy implications.** Do we need to add, change or remove policies to take this action?

Source: Norfolk School Board.

The White Bear Lake, Minnesota, school district is made up of six communities in an exurb 10 miles north of St. Paul. The board has had the full spectrum of political views, but has remained a nonpartisan body of seven with a history of reaching consensus and working with longtime superintendents.

"It's important that our employees and community feel that we have unanimity in direction," said Rolf Parsons, a board member since 1996 and a former chair. "That comes from our referendums and trying to get money for the school. We have to show we have adult leadership. It's not a rubber stamp; it's a norm."

Every meeting starts with a celebration of student accomplishment. The administration uses data from the state tests and from quarterly assessments (Measures of Academic Progress) and, with the board, has gone through three rounds of goal setting. "Every time student achievement has been number one, and fiscal responsibility is number two,"

BOX 5.1

Benchmarks and Questions for Communication and Engagement

Communicates with and engages the community by:

a) Distributing relevant information about the district.

   i)   Has the board adopted policies aimed at effective community engagement?

   ii) How does the board identify key communicator groups, and how are these groups utilized to disseminate district information?

   iii) What venues are used to promote the achievements of students?

   iv) Do board members clearly understand the key messages the board is trying to convey?

   v)   How well trained is each board member on media relations?

b) Providing methods of communication to the board and appropriate staff.

   i)   What policies has the board adopted to encourage and provide for communication between the board, the staff, and the community?

   ii) How have these policies been communicated to all interested parties?

   iii) What forums are provided for community input to the staff and the board?

---

said Parsons. There are twenty-four meetings a year. Every fourth meeting is a work-study meeting, or an informal meeting with the superintendent and his five cabinet officers and selected staff to talk about a particular topic, like negotiations.

"We have a very talented board," said Parsons. "Our challenge is finance." Due to falling enrollments, the district has had to make $10 million in budget cuts since 2003.

The board has made it a practice to use focus groups to communicate the need for financial support and to get guidance on where to make

c) Seeking input through a variety of methods.

   i)   How are adopted policies governing public participation at board meetings communicated to the public in addition to being available at board meetings?

   ii) How does the board use established community advisory committees to provide input into its decision making?

   iii) How do the board and the staff utilize the district Web site as a communication tool?

   iv) Does the board use a survey tool to solicit input, as necessary?

   v)   How are constituents' views solicited to ensure that all views are represented?

d) Including stakeholders in all communications.

   i)   Has the board developed a plan to identify stakeholders and appropriate methods for communication with them?

   ii) Has the board adopted a policy for distribution of materials and information to appropriate stakeholders?

   iii) Does the board have a process for presenting information about the school district to various community and civic organizations?

   iv) Does the board communicate in a succinct manner that is understandable?

   v)   Do board meetings include an opportunity for students and staff to make presentations?

Source: Pennsylvania School Boards Association.

cuts. "It's just been a tremendous safety valve; the community input has changed the board's opinions," he said.

Focus groups have been especially beneficial in making tough decisions among several top priorities competing for scarce resources. "Twice we've had proposals [from the superintendent] to cut back on student transportation," Parsons explained. "In Wisconsin, the state funds transportation for students who live two or more miles away. We have funded transportation for anyone living one mile or more. Any dollar you save for transportation is money for the classroom. However, student safety is one of the board's goals." A principal's son was hit while walking to school along a local highway, so the topic is a sensitive one for the community, he said.

Focus groups held for this issue in 2007 were well attended, said Parsons. Many parents who turned out to speak said they were willing to pay $200 a year in transportation fees in order to maintain classroom resources. "We gave that very serious thought," said Parsons, "but once the focus groups were over, our phones started ringing; the people who work nights and can't come to meetings called us up and said, I don't have $200."

Eventually, the board decided not to charge fees. Still, Parsons thinks the focus groups worked to get the attention of the community about the choice that needed to be made.

Focus groups have also been used by the board and the district before introducing new initiatives in the schools. A year was spent doing focus groups before approving a new math curriculum, and again before adopting a new social studies curriculum. "You can't lose by asking people's opinion; we see our role as being bridges," he said.

Many boards also employ more old-fashioned techniques to communicate. Assigning members to be "liaisons" to individual schools for events or to be emissaries to major community organizations, like the chamber of commerce or a local university, is another way a school board can build in regular contacts with the community.

In addition to traditional face-to-face meetings and mailings, technology is providing many ways to communicate directly with stakeholders. It used to be that boards and school districts were dependent on local newspapers to get information out. But those days are over. Web sites, e-mail lists, electronic newsletters, district blogs, automated calling, polls and Internet surveys—all are enhancing the ways boards can communicate and interact with the public.

In Tukwila, Washington, the board turned lemons into lemonade when, following a controversial walkout by students at the high school to protest the Iraq War, e-mails of those who wrote to the board were compiled for use in sending out e-newsletters.

Although technology is giving boards more options for communicating and engaging the public, most board members say that they always struggle to do more. You can never communicate enough, they say.

The important thing is to keep trying.

CHAPTER SIX

Looking Ahead

Shared Leadership   Recruiting   Sustaining

BLOOMFIELD, CT • NORFOLK, VA • LA CROSSE, WI •
ATLANTA, GA • CALVERT COUNTY, MD

For years individual members of the Bloomfield, Connecticut, school
board had flirted with the idea of establishing a uniform policy for
the town's elementary schools to better manage student behavior and
encourage an academic atmosphere similar to that of private schools
requiring uniforms. When the idea surfaced again in 2004, board members asked the parent teacher organization (PTO) to conduct a survey
to assess the level of support for the policy among the parent population. The result revealed overwhelming support for the policy. A year
later, after consulting with the PTO, the superintendent, and its lawyer,
the school board enacted a dress code requiring students in all three elementary schools to wear khaki, navy, or black pants or jumpers, and
shirts that are white or the school color. A similar process was followed
to develop and implement a uniform policy in the middle school in the
2008–09 school year and to study and approve a policy for the high
school level, which the board approved in April 2009.

Bloomfield board chair James Michel says the board's partnership
with the PTO to research the new policies worked to get stakeholders
on board with the change. "Parents were in a much better position to

do this than the board," he said. "It's human nature. It's easier to accept change when you are a part of creating it."

SHARED LEADERSHIP

The uniform policy itself may not seem like a breakthrough idea. Many districts have tried these policies. The way the Bloomfield board went about crafting the new policy is unique. And it's but one example of how high-functioning boards are including community members and groups like the local PTO in their work to solve problems and build support for school change directed at student achievement.

Unlike communication and engagement, shared leadership implies more of a two-way interaction rather than a one-way conveying of information, or convincing community members to help with an existing project. It implies that others outside the school board and superintendent play a role in helping shape decisions in the district. Sharing leadership is not just a tool to help others understand initiatives. As Michel noted, it also helps increase the chances that those others, because they participated in creating something, will have a stake in whether it succeeds, and thus will help to make sure it does. This is commonly referred to as *buy-in*, or a way to get "everyone on the same page" or "everyone rowing in the same direction."

Sharing leadership helps others who have a stake in improved student achievement—like parents, local employers, and taxpayers who may not have children but who still foot the bill for schools—to buy into district initiatives, thus increasing the odds that initiatives will be sustained. Sustaining initiatives is important because changes in education take time—five years or more—to bear fruit and take hold within institutions like schools and school districts.[1] Shared leadership can also lead to long-term partnerships with community groups that can provide needed financial and other resources to the district down the road.

Shared leadership is different from "classical" or traditional leadership in that it encourages transparent and open exchange of information, shared responsibility for problems and solutions, and opportunities for learning that will allow others to contribute.[2]

Although shared leadership is desirable because it leads to more effective governance, it does not mean the board is relinquishing its governance role, and that should be made clear, counsels the National School Boards Association. "Although shared decision making widens the circle of input from others with an interest and responsibility for student learning, it does not change the board's authority, responsibility, and accountability for decisions," the association states in its workbook, *Targeting Student Learning: The School Board's Role as Policymaker.*[3]

To be sure, school boards share leadership in different ways. As mentioned in early chapters, the Boston School Committee has appointed community members to serve as cochairs of ad hoc task forces, such as the one formed to recommend changes to its student assignment system. The Montgomery, Alabama, school board and superintendent agreed on a five-year strategic plan crafted in part with members of the chamber of commerce, who are helping to create vocational academies in the city's high schools. In Madison County, Kentucky, the board is working with the Kentucky Department of Education to partner with its sixteen school-based school councils on a model of shared governance to review student data and discuss how councils, which have power of hiring and curriculum in individual school buildings, can assist with the district's initiatives to raise achievement for all students. The Norfolk, Virginia, school board employed a panel of citizens to review a recommendation for a comprehensive facilities plan.

Norfolk has also gone further to include members of its PTO in its work with the Panasonic Foundation to increase the achievement of disadvantaged students in the system. Members of the PTO accompany Norfolk board members, administrators, principals, and teacher association leaders to off-site meetings sponsored annually by the foundation. The idea is to give the school teams a concentrated period of time—a long weekend—to work on the three "achievable goals" that the districts have chosen to work on for the year, says Andrew Gelber of the Panasonic Foundation.

Board chair Barry Bishop says different representatives from these groups go each time so that more people can participate. He believes this has helped build trust across the school district. "Absent that, it is so difficult to accomplish what we want to accomplish and create common goals," he said.

Boards that use the policy governance model (see chapter 3) are required to hold regular "linkages" with community groups, not just to communicate, but as part of the process of continually assessing the board's goals and forming ideas for future goals.

Linkages have really "opened the board to specific ideas from the groups" and "been really good for focusing the board on policies and student achievement," according to La Crosse, Wisconsin, board president Christine Clair. "Once very five or six weeks, we meet with a group not so much to talk, but listen to what they have to say, about how they feel our education system is doing for students, how they think we might do better," said Clair. "At the next board meeting, we talk about what we learned at those linkages, and we talk about whether we need to amend our policies." Among the groups that the board meets with are school staff, local legislators, local government officials, the district-wide parent committee, the local business association, and high school students.

At a meeting held in 2008, a group of high school juniors and seniors appealed to the board to find ways to give them more opportunities to go to job sites and work to get hands-on experience—for example, a hospital placement to supplement what they are learning in biology class. As a result, the district is setting up specialized academies for high schoolers—the first, a health science academy, will open in the fall of 2009—and matching students with mentors working in the field who they can "shadow."

RECRUITING THE RIGHT MEMBERS

High-functioning boards are not only proactive about reaching out to the community for input into decisions. There also comes a point when they face the prospect of turnover among their members and must turn to the community for help with continuity of leadership.

It's not unusual to find that when a district is on the upswing and there is a good, collaborative relationship between the superintendent and the school board, the prospect of board turnover can be extremely anxiety provoking. The superintendent wonders whether the new board will be supportive of agreed-upon policies and initiatives. Even high-functioning boards can face the prospect of candidates who may care more about a single issue (taxes, the science curriculum, and vouchers are some of the more traditional ones) than about working with their colleagues to support a multiyear strategic plan that has been carefully crafted and enjoys wide support.

As it turns out, high-functioning boards give some serious thought to board continuity well before election time. Many members interviewed for this book say they believe that part of their duty as a board member is to encourage and recruit future board members as a way of ensuring continuity and stability for those things in the district that have led to student gains.

"We need to be identifying some good people to run for the school board instead of sitting back and seeing who will run," Leni Patterson of the Laurens District 55, South Carolina, school board told me. "If you really want to improve your schools, you really have to recruit. We look for parents who are real active in the schools, who want to be involved, who understand the issues, and who want to be involved for the right reason—folks who want to see our schools improve, who are not out to make our schools or the superintendent look bad. We need people who don't have a political agenda. All that does is take the focus away from student achievement."

Patterson said she has helped find community members to run for the board to replace retiring members in the last three elections. She encourages them to start attending school board meetings regularly up to a year before they run.

Who makes a good board member? Basically, anyone who cares about the education of all students in a district, who is willing to serve in a nonpartisan capacity, do the homework required before meetings, and be a team player, board members say. (See figure 6.1.)

Some boards also look to recruit citizens who can bring to the board special talents that are needed. In White Bear Lake, Minnesota, which has wrestled with the need to run referendums to maintain financial support for the schools, the board encourages active community members who have helped run levy campaigns to think about running for vacant seats, says member Rolf Parsons. "We tend to get well-connected

FIGURE 6.1 *What makes a good board member*

Whether serving on a board that is appointed or elected, veteran board members and those who work with them suggest keeping these traits in mind when recruiting new board members:

• Belief that student achievement is possible for every student

• An understanding of the value of school in strengthening a community

• Some ability to analyze data or know what it can provide

• Ability to be a critical thinker

• Need to be in it for students, not yourself

• Ability to be a team player

• Ability to listen and find common ground

board members, even those with public relations experience. You help run a levy campaign, then people know who you are."

In states and localities experiencing rapid change in demographics, school boards such as those in Tukwila, Washington, and Springdale, Arkansas, have used the opportunities presented by vacant board seats to appoint citizens who represent the diverse racial and ethnic groups in the community. This is also another way of sharing leadership, by including a wider range of stakeholders.

In addition to recruiting, high-functioning boards are involved in helping potential members understand how the school board functions, even before they are elected, as a way of providing stability and continuity in districts making student gains.

In Berlin, Connecticut, the school board sponsors a thirty-hour orientation for all school board candidates that includes informational tours led by the principals of all the Berlin schools, and a seminar run by the CABE entitled, "So You Want to Be a Board Member." Candidates learn about the roles and responsibilities of a board member, including the importance of facts about the local schools.

The orientation helped dispel misinformation that otherwise may be disseminated by candidates during the election that can be damaging to the reputation of the public schools and confusing to the public. Board president Gary Brochu said sitting school board members have noticed how the orientation has helped improve the tenor of debates at election time.

Theoretically, the hallmarks of high-achieving boards—efficient meetings, collaborative relationships, focus on student achievement rather than the minutiae of the district—should make it easier to recruit new members. In a follow-up to its 1997 study of quality governance boards published in 2000, NESDEC authors noted a shortage of candidates in some localities and urged boards to adopt practices that would make board service more attractive to citizens. "Busy Americans place an increasingly higher premium on their free time," the authors wrote. "Citizens will be more inclined to continue to serve on a school board when more time at board meetings is spent on developing goals and policies for quality education for all children and less time on administrative details such as personnel matters, bus schedules, roof repairs and selecting an athletic coach."[4]

SUSTAINING

While board continuity is important to sustaining district efforts to raise student achievement, who ends up elected or appointed to boards is not easily predicted or controlled. For that reason, high-functioning boards also seek ways to guarantee continuity of their most important initiatives, processes, and practices through a variety of means.

Typically, high-functioning districts have a multiyear plan or well-publicized goals for maintaining a focus on student achievement over time that are not easy to change unless there is dramatic turnover on the board or, perhaps, a change in superintendents.

Atlanta, for example, has a five-year strategic plan for improving student achievement. However, due to a number of factors, sustainability is a particular concern. First of all, all nine seats on the Atlanta board are up for reelection every four years, a situation that board chair LaChandra Butler Burks calls "scary." It is also a large urban system where coordination and continuity of efforts directed at student achievement for all students had not existed until recent times. Sustainability has been the focus of the work between the Panasonic Foundation and the school district as it undertakes systemic reform, said Andrew Gelber, a Panasonic senior consultant who has worked with the Atlanta Public Schools. "We talk about institutionalizing a way of working," he said, explaining that to institutionalize something means putting a process or practice in writing and, typically, making it a policy that is voted on by the board, he said. (See figure 6.2.)

For its part, the Atlanta board has focused its sustainability efforts on communication. After drafting and enacted into policy its norms and values document to guide the ways board members would communicate with each other, the board turned its attention to processes for communicating with the superintendent and staff. One product of those discussions was a work session calendar of topics related to the district goals that board members wanted to monitor during the year. The board believed in the need for aligning its work with the goals, but didn't have a process in place to make that happen until the work session calendar was created, said Gelber.

As board chair, Butler Burks asked each board member to rank order items on the strategic plan that they were interested in monitoring or knowing more about. Using this information, Butler Burks created a calendar requiring two reports per month from staff to be discussed in work sessions during the board's Committee of the Whole meetings.

FIGURE 6.2 *Sustaining the work*

Strategies that high-functioning boards use to "institutionalize" processes that help focus the board and other stakeholders on student achievement and maintain continuity of efforts to reach achievement goals are:

- Norms and values policies and codes of conduct
- Multiyear goals and strategic plans
- Multiyear projected budgets
- Annual board self-evaluations
- Communication policies
- Candidate orientations
- School board handbooks

The calendar system also "keeps the board focused to keep the staff working on student achievement," she said.

The system also promotes a collaborative relationship with the administration, said Gelber: "Basically, the board said, there are things that are going to come up that are unpredictable, but we already know the main things that we want to keep track of." The calendar of reports to be given during monthly work sessions helps the administration as well, he said, since it gives the administration time to anticipate and plan for each month's set of reports. "The calendar releases the administration to do a really, really good job about pulling things together," said Gelber.

The board has also institutionalized a way of fielding questions from board members before voting meetings. Written materials are disseminated from the superintendent to board members before the meetings, and members are responsible for sending questions for the superintendent electronically to the chair. The questions are compiled and sent to the superintendent in advance of the meeting so she will be prepared to answer them. The board, said Gelber, "is coming to see this process as a collaborative process and becoming convinced of the idea that they will get the most out of presentations if they help the administration to do that well."

Finally, the board is working to institutionalize new channels of communications to stakeholders. In workshops with Panasonic facilitators, the board developed the idea for a new electronic newsletter, called the E-Blast, to "make current what the board is focusing on and make it immediately available to lots and lots of people," said Gelber.

Also, because in Atlanta different board members are elected from different parts of the city, the board is grappling with how to customize information about districtwide reform initiatives, to highlight aspects that pertain to the schools in their part of the city, said Gelber. The need emerged out of the different questions each board member was fielding about the high school reform effort, in which Atlanta's large high schools are being broken up into smaller schools and academies over a five-year period. In addition to the common talking points developed about the high school reform initiative in general, each member will work with the administration to create talking points about how the reform effort will affect their own geographic zone.

Finally, in addition to creating and institutionalizing board processes, the Atlanta board has sought to sustain the district's most important school reforms by "turning them into policy," said board chair Butler Burks. Major reform initiatives like the $64 million high school initiative, for example, not only are voted on by the board, but, upon passage, are converted to formal resolutions that are then voted on by the board and signed by the chair. Resolutions are common on boards as a formal way of recognizing individuals and groups for good works, but not so commonly employed for reform initiatives.

"We think it's a little unique," said Butler Burks. "We found this way to show the board support. Because it's adopted by the full board, we think it addresses the issue of sustainability. If [superintendent] Hall were to leave today, the high school reform plan has been voted as a five-year plan. Any new superintendent would have to continue it. It's embedded," she said.

So far, the initiative shows signs of success. At the first high school converted to small schools—Carver High School—graduation rates have increased from 23 percent to 74 percent. The graduation rate projected for the first cohort to go all the way through the new small school is over 80 percent, said Butler Burks. "When you have success like that, you don't want someone new coming in with the next 'great idea.' That's what happened to us before Dr. Hall came. We want to make sure the reform models that are working stay in place."

Also, 2009 was the first year the board voted for a five-year projected budget in addition to an annual budget, she said. "We thought it was important because a lot of our initiatives are spread across four or five years, and we need a financial document that supports those over four or five years."

Among the most impressive efforts at sustainability among the boards interviewed for this book is the handbook written and published by the Calvert County, Maryland, Board of Education in 2008. The fifty-eight-page guide is a virtual bible of everything a new board member might conceivably need to know about how the board operates—everything from the legal implications of arbitrary policy changes to information on how to pick up their mail.

The handbook was written when the board faced the certain prospect of a turnover of a majority of its five members at the end of 2008, when the board chair retired and two other members were prohibited by term limitations from running again. The board, which had been an appointed body prior to 1996, decided to write down the nuts and bolts of serving on the elected board, as well as the norms and values that they felt had led to sustained gains in student achievement during their tenure.

In the introduction to the handbook, entitled "Purpose," the members wrote, "The ability to consistently provide the leadership necessary for a first-class public school system has been aided through the board's ability to remain consistent in its basic manner of operations. This has provided the stability that is the foundation of long-term sustained success."[5]

Fittingly, for a board with sustainability on its mind, the group challenged board members who come after them to continue the handbook tradition: "It is expected that this is a living document that will stimulate questions, serve as a guidepost, and be updated as the needs of the Board and community dictate in the years ahead. To that end, each Board will provide a written legacy to its successors to ensure that future transitions of leadership will be done in a measured, steady manner to preserve and enhance the excellence of educational opportunity offered to our students, parents and community." The document embodies the practices and beliefs that have made the Calvert County school board successful, said superintendent Jack Smith. "They are the rules they live by; they are the norms of the group."

La Crosse School Profile

CENTRAL HIGH SCHOOL
SCHOOL PROFILE
Evidence of Success 2007-08

District Mission (E1):
Students will discover their talents and abilities and will be prepared to pursue their dreams and aspirations while contributing effectively to their local, national and global communities.

Leadership:
Administrative Staff =
Thomas Barth, PRINCIPAL
Joe Beran, ACTIVITIES DIRECTOR
Troy McDonald, ASSOCIATE PRINCIPAL
Jeff Fleig, ASSOCIATE PRINCIPAL

Key Committees =
Site Plan
Behavior Council
Technology
Staff Development
Academic Intervention Team
Co-curricular
Department Chairs

School Day/Learning Time:
Hours: 7:40 a.m.-3:20 p.m.
M, Th, F: 8 - 50 minute periods
T, W: 4 - 85 minute periods with a 30 minute resource time

After-School Hours:
Co-curricular until 10:00 p.m.

Summer School Options:
Health
Physical Education
Photography
Zoology
Novanet – credit recovery

Staff:
Certified Staff = 91.61
Teacher Asst. = 15.78
Secretaries = 8

Average Class Size
Core Classes = 27
Elective Classes = 23

Student Demographics:
Source: May 2008 Data Mining Report

Year	'07-'08	'06-'07
Total Enrolled =	1256	1321
Afr-Am =	3.7% (47)	3.6% (48)
Nat-Am =	0.6% (8)	0.9% (12)
Caucasian =	82.2% (1032)	81.4% (1075)
Hispanic =	1.4% (18)	1.2% (16)
Asian-Am =	12% (151)	12.9% (170)
Free/Reduced =	29.8%	28.9%

School Programs:
Comprehensive 9-12 curriculum including a variety of Advanced Placement classes.

Skills Classes – Meet the needs of the challenged learner.
Success Center - First step academic help program for at-risk or potentially at-risk students.
Transition - Programs are in place to ease transitions for new students and incoming 9th graders who benefit from strong middle and high school collaborations (Link Crew). One program involved Central Administrators and teachers putting on programs in the middle school.
Adacemic Intervention Team – Program that identifies 9th grade students who were struggling academically. Staff monitored students individually.
PLTW – Pre-Engineering high school program

Unique School Programs/Accomplishments
Things We're Most Proud Of:
- 308 students were honored by the School Board for Academic Excellence earning a 3.5 or above grade point average.
- Memorial Day Program is in its 86th year.
- Perfect Attendance and Student of the Month Recognition
- Transition Program for Freshmen – Link Crew
- Grand Central Station has won 39 competitions throughout the Midwest since 1996.
- Wind Ensemble selected to perform at State Music Convention
- Friday Night Live Program to provide a positive evening alternative for students
- Baseball Team qualified for the State Tournament
- Champions – Peer Mentoring Program
- Academic Intervention Team
- J A Titan – National Economics Champion – third time in five years
- Extended Learning Day Schedule

HIGH ACADEMIC STANDARDS:
E2:-Students will demonstrate a high level of individual success in all required and elective academic/curricular areas using multiple measures of performance.

● School Performance Data for:	'07-'08	'06-'07	'05-'06	'04-'05
Attendance	Not avail.	96.7%	96.8%	96.7%
% Profic+Adv in: 10th Gr. Reading	70%	70%	79%	73%
% Profic+Adv in: 10th Gr. Lang. Arts	64%	71%	76%	69%
% Profic+Adv in: 10th Gr. Math	72%	71%	79%	73%
% Profic+Adv in: 10th Gr. Science	78%	78%	74%	76%
% Profic+Adv in: 10th Gr. Soc Studies	80%	78%	83%	76%
Retentions	Not avail.	0.9% (11)	1.2% (15)	1.8% (25)
Suspensions	Not avail.	5.2% (69)	5.5% (72)	7.7% (105)
Expulsions	Not avail.	0	0	0.3% (4)
% Not Tested (Reading):	1%	1%	1%	1%
Met Adequate Yearly Progress (AYP)	Yes	Yes	Yes	Yes

● **Curriculum-Based Achievement Indicators**
Example: Products, performances, grades, school assessment data, etc.
- Two National Merit Scholarship Finalists and one Commended Student.
- AP Scores above State and National averages.
- Students qualified for National History Day Competition.

● **Academics Outside School Day**
- International student travel to Germany, Mexico, China, and Belize
- Co-op Programs in Marketing, HERO, and Technology Education
- Mentorship Program
- Alternative Pathways
- County Youth Initiative
- State medal winners in French and German Speaking Contests
- All instrumental and choral groups received Division I ratings at District Large Group Contest.
- Central music students consistently win exemplary performer awards at State music contests.
- Grand Central Station has won numerous best choreography, best vocal, and best back-up band awards at competitions.
- Four students participated in State Forensics Competition.
- FBLA State Regional Vice-President
- On-line ACT Prep Program
- Mock Trial Team qualified for State Competition
- PLAN Test

CENTRAL HIGH SCHOOL – Page 2
Evidence of Success **2007-08**

School Goals:

1. Maintain a historical one to two percentage points above the state average in all areas of the WKCE Test.
2. Decrease the overall percentage of ninth grade students who have failed a core area course by 5%.

Professional Development:

- All teachers received website development training.
- Many teachers completed training in a course designed to understand students in poverty.
- Staff members participated in two book studies.

Family, School, and Community Partnerships:

La Crosse Education Foundation
- Helps with grants to support students in need through the Random Act of Kindness Fund.

Mentorships/Apprenticeships/Co-Ops
- Employers work in partnership to offer Central students work opportunities and experience in the community.

Central Booster Club
- "Yes You Can" can collection
- Scholarships
- Financial Support

Central Alumni Association
- Scholarships - $8,000 in 2007-08
- Work together on Alumni events such as nt, Alumni Directory and Hall of Excellence.

Hall of Excellence
- Originated in 1999
- Honors alumni and staff for outstanding achievement or service to Central High School or the community they reside in.

School Meetings
- Meetings with parents representing each school class, transition meetings, financial aid meetings with senior parents, curriculum fair, and co-curricular meetings.

Parent Organizations
- Organization supporting band, show choir, and co-curricular teams.

Altra Federal Credit Union
- Branch office at Central.

- College & Military Visits

- Job Shadows & Career Speakers from the Community

- Hosted Big Family New Years Eve Party

STANDARDS OF THE HEART – caring, success, potential

E3: Students will strive for mutual understanding as contributing citizens in a diverse world.

E4: Students will acquire the knowledge and skills necessary to make effective and responsible life choices.

- **Core Values/Citizenship Education**
  - Central High School students participated in Government Day.
  - Student Senate and National Honor Society Food Drives.
  - Miracle Minute Fund-raisers for Autism and China
  - Rotary Lights Participation
  - National Honor Society held four blood drives.
  - Peer P.A.S.S. Tutors
  - Annual Red Raider Rock-A-Thon Fund-raiser
  - Kula Walk
  - Show Choir Benefit for St. Claire Health Mission

- **Student Services**
  - Central High School has four counselors, a school psychologist, and a school social worker.
  - Academic, career, and personal/crisis counseling.
  - Facilitate and interpret a wide variety of tests.
  - Each student develops a four year high school plan.
  - Career assistant available to coordinate career speakers and job shadows.
  - Student support groups.
  - Evening informational meetings for parents.

- **Community Involvement/Volunteer Work**
  - Student Senate Rock-A-Thon
  - Student Senate volunteer work at Community Food Pantry.
  - NHS Volunteer Work
  - Central music students are active in a larger community through their involvement in recitals, singing competitions, La Crosse Youth Symphony and La Crosse Concert Band.
  - Pumpkin Pie baking for Thanksgiving Day Program

- **Assemblies/School-Wide Efforts**
  - Olympic Week Talent Night
  - Pep Assemblies
  - Academic Excellence Recognition
  - Opening Day Welcome Back Assembly
  - Senior Assembly – Fire Safety
  - Senior Appreciation Lunch
  - Friday Night Live Recreation Nights
  - School Leader assembly
  - 9th Grade Welcome Program
  - Ninth grade students received Diversity training.

- **Clubs, Co-Ex Activities**
  - Central High School offers a wide array of co-curricular activities ranging from music, to athletes, to intramurals. Over 850 students participate in athletics and 325 participating in non-athletic groups annually.
  - Central has been rich in athletic and co-curricular tradition.
  - Intramural Bowling, Volleyball & Open Gym

Source: School District of La Crosse, http://www.lacrosseschools.com.

Norfolk Data Dashboard

Superintendent of Schools
Dr. Stephen C. Jones
757-628-3838, Telephone
757-628-3820, Fax

Number of Professional Teaching Contracts: 3,612 (Sept. 30th, 2007)

Sept. 30th, 2007 Membership

Student Enrollment	35,136
African American	63.9%
Asian	2.4%
Hispanic	3.9%
American Indian	0.2%
White	23.7%
Other	6.0%
Female	48.6%
Male	51.4%
Regular Education (Sept. 30)	86.7%
Special Education (Sept. 30)	13.3%
Gifted Education (spring)	10.5%
Free-Reduced Meals	59.3%
Stability of Students 2007–2008	82.%
Per Pupil Expenditure	$8,500

State and Division Level Indicators (Tier 1)

Indicator – Tier 1 data for 2006-07 will be completed no later than November 2007 and on this same schedule in subsequent years.	Virginia Percent Passing			Norfolk Percent Passing			Norfolk - #/% Tested			NPS Benchmark
	05-06	06-07	07-08	05-06	06-07	07-08	05-06	06-07	07-08	07-08
Continuous Growth of Student Academic Achievement										
Percent proficient or better in SOL elementary school areas										
Grade 3										
English/Reading	84	80	84	77	76	78	2,494/98%	2,608/99.7%	2,622/99.6%	75%
Mathematics	90	89	89	87	86	87	2,491/98%	2,605/99.8%	2,618/99.9%	70%
History/Social Science	91	92	93	93	90	89	2,407/95%	2,498/96%	2,567/98.1%	50%
Science	90	88	88	86	83	82	2,412/95%	2,516/96%	2,594/98.7%	50%
Grade 4										
English/Reading	86	87	88	86	85	84	2,203/97%	2,349/99%	2,468/99.7%	70%
Mathematics	77	81	84	74	78	79	2,352/98%	2,362/99.7%	2,478/99.9%	70%
Grade 5										
English/Reading	87	87	89	82	88	87	2,474/97%	2,442/99.6%	2,239/99.6%	75%
Writing	89	89	87	91	90	83	2,434/96%	2,401/97.2%	2,231/98.2%	70%
Mathematics	83	87	88	85	87	87	2,493/98%	2,443/99.5%	2,250/99.9%	70%
History/Social Science	85	92	90	83	93	92	2,382/94%	2,364/97%	2,183/96.9%	70%
Science	85	88	88	80	87	86	2,376/93%	2,370/96%	2,235/98.9%	70%

State and Division Level Indicators (Tier 1)

Indicator – Tier 1 data for 2007-08 will be completed no later than November 2008 and on this same schedule in subsequent years.	Virginia Percent Passing			Norfolk Percent Passing			Norfolk – #/% Tested			NPS Benchmark
	05-06	06-07	07-08	05-06	06-07	07-08	05-06	06-07	07-08	07-08

Continuous Growth of Student Academic Achievement

Percent proficient or better in SOL middle school areas

Indicator	Virginia 05-06	Virginia 06-07	Virginia 07-08	Norfolk 05-06	Norfolk 06-07	Norfolk 07-08	Tested 05-06	Tested 06-07	Tested 07-08	NPS Benchmark 07-08
English 6	83	84	85	70	79	75	2,323/94%	2,253/987%	2,189/97%	70%
Mathematics 6	51	60	68	34	49	58	2,328/94%	2,252/98%	2,206/98%	70%
English 7	81	82	86	70	74	81	2,560/93%	2,368/97%	2,165/96%	70%
Mathematics 7	44	56	65	29	43	53	2,564/93%	2,245/97%	2,040/96%	70%
English 8	78	80	83	74	70	68	2,327/91%	2,396/96%	2,291/97%	70%
Writing 8	91	86	87	91	79	81	2,235/90%	2,365/93%	2,265/96%	70%
Mathematics 8	76	77	83	71	61	66	2,325/89%	2,283/96%	2,149/96%	70%
History/Social Science 8	81	81	83	81	79	76	2,263/92%	2,238/94%	2,209/97%	70%
Science 8	87	89	90	82	79	83	2,286/89%	2,312/78%	2,557/98%	70%
Algebra I (VA includes h.s. scores)	81	92	93	81	84	86	942/100%	1,161/100%	2,539/97%	70%
Geometry (VA includes h.s. scores)	76	86	87	73	78	80	260/100%	334/100%	2,063/99%	70%
Earth Science (VA includes h.s. scores)	70	85	86	78	80	78	392/100%	428/100%	2,029/96%	70%
Biology (VA includes h.s. scores)	73	87	88	73	85	84	269/100%	248/100%	2,238/97%	70%

State and Division Level Indicators (Tier 1)

Indicator – Tier 1 data for 2007-08 will be completed no later than November 2008 and on this same schedule in subsequent years.	Virginia Percent Passing			Norfolk Percent Passing			Norfolk - #/% Tested			NPS Benchmark
	05-06	06-07	07-08	05-06	06-07	07-08	05-06	06-07	07-08	07-08
Continuous Growth of Student Academic Achievement										
Percent proficient or better in SOL End-Of-Course high school areas										
English	90	94	94	91	93	94	1,656/98%	1,535/98%	1,656/99%	70%
Writing	88	92	92	87	94	92	1,584/96%	1,592/96%	1,678/97%	70%
Algebra I (VA includes m.s. scores)	88	92	93	81	84	86	1,395/96%	1,592/95%	2,539/97%	70%
Geometry (VA includes m.s. scores)	83	86	87	73	78	80	1,638/98%	1,588/97%	2,063/99%	70%
Algebra II	85	88	90	84	84	85	1,095/99%	1,219/98%	1,328/99%	70%
Earth Science (VA includes m.s. scores)	82	85	86	78	80	78	1,474/95%	1,666/94%	2,029/96%	70%
Biology (VA includes m.s. scores)	83	87	88	73	85	84	2,398/95%	1,484/93%	2,385/97%	70%
Chemistry	87	91	92	91	94	91	842/99%	918/97%	1,002/99%	70%
World Geography	77	83	84	75	83	96	612/95%	358/97%	328/99%	70%
World History to 1500 AD	85	89	91	77	86	85	1,900/96%	1,787/95%	2,178/96%	70%
World History 1500 to Present	89	92	92	84	87	86	1,150/95%	1,499/95%	1,327/95%	70%
Virginia & U.S. History	92	93	94	91	90	93	1,758/95%	1,843/94%	1,694/96%	70%

Continuous Growth of Student Academic Achievement										
Indicator – Tier 1 data for 2007-08 will be completed no later than November 2008 and on this same schedule in subsequent years.	Virginia			Norfolk			Norfolk - #/% Tested			NPS Benchmark
	05-06	06-07	07-08	05-06	06-07	07-08	05-06	06-07	07-08	07-08
Percentage of graduates taking SAT				53.6%	56.8%	49.3%	1,507/54%	1,649/57%	1,748/49%	
Average Scores on SAT by graduates										
Mathematics	512	511	511	455	449	450	802/53%	961/59%	856/49%	
Critical Reading	513	511	512	456	452	457	802/53%	961/59%	856/49%	
Writing	500	498	499	452	438	442	802/53%	961/59%	856/49%	
Average of highest scores by graduates - SAT										
Mathematics				461	458	455				
Critical Reading				462	460	463				
Writing				458	447	447				
Percentage of grade 11 students taking PSAT				69.5%	67.2%	70.7%				
Average scores of graduating seniors on ACT										
Mathematics	21.0	21.2	21.8	17.5	17.6	18.0				
English	20.6	21.0	21.5	16.5	15.7	16.7				
Number or % of graduates taking ACT	9,182	14,653	16,896	16%	16%	17.6				
Percentage of students enrolled in:										
Advanced Placement course enrollment				1,711	1,829	1,838	81.2%	82.8%	95.8%	
Dual Enrollment courses (**Maury & Norview HS - 11,12**)				1.8%	2.1%	0.9%				
International Baccalaureate courses (**Granby HS**)				9.4%	8.9%	11.1%				

Continuous Growth of Student Academic Achievement (continued)

Indicator – Tier 1 data for 2007-08 will be completed no later than November 2008 and on this same schedule in subsequent years.	Virginia			Norfolk			Norfolk - #/% Tested			NPS Benchmark
	05-06	06-07	07-08	05-06	06-07	07-08	05-06	06-07	07-08	07-08
Governor's School				0.98%	0.52%	1.24%				
Passing rates of students enrolled in:										
Advanced Placement (score of 3 or more)				619 (44.6%)	679 (43.6%)	693 (39.4%)				
Dual Enrollment courses (Maury & Norview HS –11,12)				94.7%	89.7%	86.6%				
International Baccalaureate Courses				98.9%	96.4%	96.3%				
Governor's School				100%	99.5%	99.1%				

	Division Score			#/% Tested			Division Goal
	05-06	06-07	07-08	05-06	06-07	07-08	07-08
Percentage of students who met or exceeded benchmarks as measured by the Phonemic Awareness and Literacy Screening (PALS)							
Kindergarten	86%	83%	86%	2,432/78%	2,957/100%	2,917/97%	
Grade 1	81%	82%	82%	2,248/75%	2,973/99%	2,806/98%	
Percent of students reading at or above grade level (STAR Reading Test - Sept. 30th membership used as denominator)							
Grade 3	61.6%	56.6%	57.0%	2,416/94%	2,424/90%	2,574/96%	
Percentage of students reading at or above grade level in grade 8 (Gates MacGinitie Reading Test)							
Grade 5 Vocabulary	58.1%	56.1%	55.7%				
Comprehension	61.1%	54.9%	54.2%				
Grade 8 Vocabulary	59.8%	56.3%	55.0%				
Comprehension	47.6%	57.7%	55.2%				

Continuous Growth of Student Academic Achievement *(continued)*

Indicator – Tier 1 data for 2007-08 will be completed no later than November 2008 and on this same schedule in subsequent years.	Division Score			#/% Tested			Division Goal 07-08
	05-06	**06-07**	**07-08**				
Percent of students promoted							
Elementary Schools	94%	95%	98%				
Middle Schools	77%	77%	80%				
High Schools	64%	66%	68%				
Average daily percent of attendance of students							
Elementary Schools	96%	96%	96%				
Middle Schools	93%	93%	93%				
High Schools	91%	91%	89%				

State and Division Level Indicators (Tier 1)

	Division Score			#/% Tested			Division Goal 07-08
	05-06	**06-07**	**07-08**	**05-06**	**06-07**	**07-08**	
Percentage of students missing 10 or more days							
Elementary Schools	20.4%	20.2%	20.8%				Decrease
Middle Schools	36.0%	35.3%	32.2%				Decrease
High Schools	45.4%	45.7%	44.6%				Decrease
Student drop out rate							
Middle Schools	0.99%	1.05%	1.31%				Decrease
High Schools	2.58%	4.28%	5.34%				Decrease
Graduation rate (changed per NCLB requirements)	78.29%	80.44%	75.67%				Increase

State and Division Level Indicators (Tier 1) *(continued)*

Indicator – Tier 1 data for 2007-08 will be completed no later than November 2008 and on this same schedule in subsequent years.	05-06	06-07	07-08	Division Goal 07-08
Percentage of students in grade 9 who completed an approved program 4 yrs in NPS (disregarding those students who transfer to a school outside NPS) **(Changed per VA NCLB req.)**	88.3%	90.1%	88.4%	Increase
Percent of teachers meeting state licensure requirements for subjects that they teach	94%	94%	97%	Increase
Percent of secondary courses taught by subject certified teachers	94%	94%	96%	Increase
Percent of special education positions occupied by teachers with special education certification	84%	91%	96%	Increase
Percent of gifted offerings taught by teachers with matching endorsement along with appropriate content endorsement	95%	95%	92%	Increase
Professional development participant hours and percent of professional staff involved in activities based on school's focus and related to student academic achievement	79,728	78,038	98,243	Increase

Safe, Secure, and Disciplined Teaching and Learning Environment

Number of offenses against students	203	184	155	Decrease
Percent of students without incidents of physical violence in school	99.4%	99.5%	99.6%	Increase
Professional development participant hours and percent of professional staff involved in activities based on school focus and related to school climate and discipline	21,887	27,186	24,790	Increase
Number of incidents of possession of firearms in school	2	1	0	Decrease
Percent of students without incidents of possession of firearms in school	99 %	99.9%	100%	Increase
Number of incidents of weapons offenses	103	89	105	Decrease
Percent of students without incidents of possession of weapons other than firearms in school	99.7%	99.8%	99.7%	Increase

Safe, Secure, and Disciplined Teaching and Learning Environment *(continued)*

	05-06	06-07	07-08		Division Goal 07-08
Norfolk District Stakeholder Survey					
Elementary school teacher results	88%	88%	N/A		Increase
Elementary school parent results	86%	75%	88%		Increase
Elementary school student results	74%	74%	76%		Increase
Norfolk District Stakeholder Survey					
Middle school teacher results	71%	63%	N/A		Increase
Middle school parent results	63%	60%	60%		Increase
Middle school student results	44%	38%	43%		Increase
Norfolk District Stakeholder Survey					
High school teacher results	82%	67%	N/A		Increase
High school parent results	66%	60%	66%		Increase
High school student results	46%	43%	45%		Increase
Active Engagement of Parents/Business/Community in Education Process					
Number of hours that parents and community members assisted schools in improving reading and mathematics proficiency	32,956	34,632	30,473		Increase
Total volunteer hours by parents and community members in schools	84,166	90,979	93,467		Increase
Number of direct, interactive parent contacts regarding student achievement	228,793	200,668	177,418		Increase
Number of training workshops provided for parents/community	1,542	1,781	1,626		Increase

Continuous Growth of Student Academic Achievement – School Year 2007-08

Percent proficient or better in SOL Tested Areas	Asian	African American	American Indian	Hispanic	White	Other
Grade 3						
English	90	73	--	81	87	86
Mathematics	90	83	--	86	95	92
History/Social Science	96	85	--	90	95	95
Science	96	76	--	82	94	92
Grade 4						
English	96	80	--	89	91	90
Mathematics	98	75	--	85	89	84
Grade 5						
English	96	83	--	83	93	89
Writing	95	80	--	79	90	83
Mathematics	97	84	--	88	93	91
History/Social Science	--	89	--	--	--	--
Science	95	81	--	84	94	96
Grade 6						
English	92	70	--	81	84	85
Mathematics	78	50	--	68	74	65
Grade 7						
English	95	76	--	83	90	89
Mathematics	79	45	--	59	67	73

Continuous Growth of Student Academic Achievement – School Year 2007-08 *(continued)*						
Percent proficient or better in SOL tested courses	Asian	African American	American Indian	Hispanic	White	Other
Grade 8						
English	86	61	--	67	84	82
Writing	92	77	--	79	88	88
Mathematics	89	59	--	75	81	78
History/Social Science	95	71	--	74	87	81
Science	96	78	--	83	93	93
Algebra I	97	83	--	88	89	91
Geometry	90	73	--	83	91	88
Earth Science	87	71	--	88	92	88
End-Of-Course Tests						
English	93	92	--	92	98	100
Writing	94	89	--	88	96	97
Algebra I	97	83	--	88	89	91
Geometry	90	73	--	83	91	88
Algebra II	92	81	--	85	89	91
Earth Science	87	71	--	88	92	88
Biology	88	78	--	84	93	92
Chemistry	100	87	--	84	97	88
World History & Geography to 1500	93	81	--	89	94	93
World History & Geography 1500 to Present	96	81	--	85	94	89
Virginia & US History	96	89	--	96	99	99
World Geography	--	95	--	92	98	100

Continuous Growth of Student Academic Achievement – School Year 2007-08 *(continued)*						
	Asian	African American	American Indian	Hispanic	White	Other
Percent of graduates taking SAT	61.4%	47.8%	100%	47.8%	49.6%	58.0%
Diversity of students enrolled in (%):						
Advanced Placement courses (grades 11,12)	6.8%	38.3%	0.2%	3.2%	46.4%	5.1%
Dual Enrollment courses	5.0%	40.0%	0	1.3%	46.5%	6.3%
International Baccalaureate courses	16.7%	31.2%	0.9%	2.6%	45.3%	3.4%
Governor's School	12.3%	32.1%	0	0.9%	50.9%	3.8%
Drop-out Rate (%)						
Middle School	0.0%	70.3%	0.0%	1.6%	26.6%	1.6%
High School	1.6%	71.8%	0.4%	4.1%	18.9%	3.2%

Source: Norfolk Public Schools, http://www.nps.k12.va.us.

Atlanta Balanced Scorecard

[red]

Objective
1.1: Improve Student Achievement

Measure

1.1.7c: Absenteeism – High Schools

Data Source: Infinite Campus

Target: 30% or less of high school students missing 10 or more days

Frequency: Quarterly*

*Quarters are defined from the opening of the students' school year.

Calculation Method: Number of students absent 10 or more days (excused and unexcused) divided by the student population at the high school level

NOTE: The data and projections will not include North and South Psychoeducational Centers, Forest Hills Academy, West End Academy and Crim Open Campus.

Supporting Initiatives:
School Improvement Plans
High School Transformation
Social Work Services
Atlanta Fulton-County Attendance Protocol
Communities In Schools
Weed and Seed
Truancy Intervention Project

Performance Analysis:

Third quarter benchmarks indicate that high schools will not meet the goal of 30% or less of high school students missing 10 or more days.

Percent of Students Absent 10 or More Days

	Semi-Annual		3rd Quarter
	2008-2009	2008-2009	2008-2009
	Quarter 1	**Quarter 2**	**Quarter 3**
High Schools	8.95%	11.24%	10.60%
Cumulative To-Date			36.86%

This target has not been met.

[green]

Objective
1.3: Increase Community Engagement

Measure

1.3.2: Targeted community groups addressed (Neighborhood Planning Units (NPUs), Faith-Based, Government, Civic, Businesses, Community-Based, Women, and Professional)

Data Source: Reports from Superintendent and Cabinet members
Target: *89*
Frequency: *Annually*
Calculation Method: *Number of community groups addressed by Superintendent and Cabinet*
Supporting Initiatives: *N/A*

Performance Analysis

The Superintendent and Cabinet members have addressed 36 targeted community groups from January through March of 2009 (see attached charts).

A total of 82 groups have been addressed to date.

This measure is on track to meet the target.

Source: Atlanta Public Schools

Berlin Board of Education Self-Evaluation

Berlin board members and administrators use these bulleted prompts to reflect on board operations during the past year.* Comments are kept anonymous and are compiled by the president of the administrators union. The board convenes in a special meeting to review the results and talk about future directions. The board structured the self-evaluation to include areas for improvement outlined in its goals for the year (see figure 3.1 in chapter 3).

Board meetings:
- Are individuals in attendance, both the public and staff, treated with respect?
- Do board agendas consist of items related to the most important work of the district?
- Are board members prepared for meetings?
- Are meetings conducted in a productive and professional manner?
- Does the board practice distributed leadership?

Comment and recommendations:

Source: Berlin Board of Education.

Relationship with superintendent and staff:

- Do board members communicate value for the work and contributions of the superintendent?
- Do board members communicate value for the work and contributions of administrators and staff?

Comment and recommendations:

Communications:

- Does the board appear to welcome and value input from the community and staff?
- Does the board look for ways to communicate with and reach out to the public?
- Do board communications—both written and verbal—align the various constituencies and engage them in support of our schools?

Comment and recommendations:

Change leadership:

- Does the board accept ownership and accountability for driving change and managing operations?
- Does the board focus on its adopted goals (student achievement, communication, resources, board development), develop appropriate measures and metrics, and utilize those goals and metrics to make decisions?
- Does the board work in partnership with the administrative leadership team to implement continuous improvement?
- Does the board align its resources and budget requests with its goals for continuous improvement and student achievement?

Comment and recommendations:

Board of education values and boardsmanship:

- Is the board able to develop consensus on its important decisions?
- Are board members committed to a single vision for the school district?
- Do board members demonstrate an understanding of their role and distinguish between their role and administrative roles?
- Does the board appear to value the contributions of each of its members?
- Do board members keep themselves informed about educational issues and issues related to their work as a board?
- Are board members, both individually and as a group, committed to their own professional development?

Comment and recommendations:

Districts at a Glance

District	Setting	Enrollment	Board type	For more information
Atlanta, GA	Urban	50,000	Elected	www.atlanta.k12.ga.us
Berlin, CT	Suburban	3,300	Elected	www.berlinschools.org
Bloomfield, CT	Urban	2,400	Elected	www.bloomfieldschools.org
Boston, MA	Urban	56,000	Appointed	www.bostonpublicschools.org
Calvert County, MD	Suburban	17,400	Elected	www.calvertnet.k12.md.us
Elk Mound, WI	Rural	1,100	Elected	www.elkmound.k12.wi.us
Gallatin County, KY	Rural	1,600	Elected	www.gallatin.k12.ky.us
La Crosse, WI	Suburban	7,000	Elected	www.lacrosseschools.com
Laurens County District 55, SC	Rural	6,100	Elected	www.laurens55.k12.sc.us
Madison County, KY	Rural	10,000	Elected	www.madison.kyschools.us
Montgomery, AL	Urban	23,000	Elected	www.mps.k12.al.us
Norfolk, VA	Urban	36,000	Appointed	www.nps.k12.va.us
Simsbury, CT	Suburban	5,000	Elected	www.simsbury.k12.ct.us
Springdale, AR	Rural	17,500	Elected	www.springdaleschools.org
Tukwila, WA	Suburban	2,700	Elected	www.tukwila.wednet.edu
White Bear Lake, MN	Suburban	8,000	Elected	www.whitebear.k12.mn.us

Additional School Board Resources

Carver Policy Governance Model: www.carvergovernance.com
Official site of this governance model offered free for use by founder John Carver. Contains useful FAQ section that explains the essential roles and practices.

Education Commission of the States: www.ecs.org
Offers a basic synopsis of the function of school boards with links to school board types and policies as well as research and reading suggestions at www.ecs.org/html/issue.asp?issueid=103

Georgia School Boards Association: www.gsba.com
Ethics for School Board Members 2004 brochure containing a sample code of ethics: www.gsba.com/publications/publications _ethics.htm

Georgia Commission for School Board Excellence
Document section contains an extensive resource list of studies and reports on effective school board governance. https://eboard.eboard solutions.com/index.aspx?S=61187

Institute for Educational Leadership: http://www.iel.org
Cosponsor with National School Boards Association of the Jacqueline P. Danzberger Memorial Lecture series on education governance, as well as other reports.

Iowa Association of School Boards: www.ia-sb.org

- IASB provides information on what it takes to be a school board candidate and how boards and board meetings function, as well as teamwork and leadership advice: www.ia-sb.org/BoardOperations.aspx
- Guide for school board officers on the role of the school board president: http://www.ia-sb.org/WorkArea/showcontent.aspx?id =5904&LangType=1033
- IASB topics of interest include board roles and responsibilities, federal advocacy, and school finance basics: www.ia-sb.org /TopicA-Z.aspx
- Lighthouse Project of the Iowa School Board Foundation: http:// www.ia-sb.org/StudentAchievement.aspx?id=436

Idaho School Boards Association Foundation: www.idsba.org
Participant in the Lighthouse multistate board training program. Sample code of ethics and board self-evaluation are at www.idsba .org/index.php?id=4

National School Boards Association (NSBA): www.nsba.org
One-stop shopping for information about elected school boards and the activities of state board associations, which make up the membership of this nonprofit advocacy organization begun in 1940. Important resources on the Web site include:

- The Key Work of School Boards framework of eight interrelated action areas to focus and guide school boards in their work: www.nsba.org/keyworks
- Overview on school governance, including a code of ethics and online board assessment tool (under "other board issues): www.nsba.org/MainMenu/Governance.ax
- Links to state board associations: http://www.nsba.org/SecondaryMenu/StateAssociations /ExecutiveDirectors.aspx
- BoardBuzz daily board blog: http://boardbuzz.nsba.org/

- *School Board News Today*: www.nsba.org/HPC/Features/AboutSBN/SBNToday.aspx
- *American School Board Journal* monthly magazine: www.asbj.com
- Center for Public Education for research, reports, and analysis on current educational issues: www.centerforpubliceducation.org

New England School Development Council: www.nesdec.org
Copublisher of *Thinking Differently: Recommendations for 21st Century School Board/Superintendent Leadership, Governance, and Teamwork for High Student Achievement.* Richard H. Goodman and William G. Zimmerman, Jr. Available online: http://www.nesdec.org/research_dev/publications.htm

Panasonic Foundation: www.panasonic.com/meca/foundation/default.asp

Pennsylvania School Board Association: http://www.psba.org
"School Board Leadership and Management: Understanding the Basics" available at: http://www.psba.org/new-members/resources/understanding-basics.asp

Texas Association of School Boards: www.tasb.org
"Good governance" section includes information on board president training.

OTHER EDUCATION RESOURCES:

American Association of School Administrators: www.aasa.org
A membership organization for more than 13,000 educational leaders, including school superintendents, AASA publishes a number of newsletters and magazines including *School Governance & Leadership*.

Association for Supervision and Curriculum Development: www.ascd.org
ASCD, an educational leadership organization with 175,000 members, publishes a variety of resources including a free daily e-newsletter called *SmartBrief*.

The Council of Chief State School Officers: www.ccsso.org
CCSSO offers thirteen e-newsletters on subjects ranging from policy and organization news to innovations in teaching methods.

The Consortium for Policy Research in Education: www.cpre.org
A consortium of researchers from seven research institutions focused on improving elementary and secondary education, CPRE offers a free e-newsletter and access to major research reports on education policy and practice.

Education Sector: www.educationsector.org
A nonprofit, nonpartisan education policy think tank promoting policies and practices for "improved student opportunities and outcomes." Offers a free email biweekly digest and major research alert.

Education Week: www.edweek.org
Weekly covering education news for subscribers. Edweek.org offers a free e-newsletter by subject and blog.

Educators for Social Responsibility: www.esrnational.org
Resources for educators including its free "E-News" newsletter.

Harvard Education Publishing Group: www.hepg.org
Covers education policy, practice, and research through a variety of media including the Harvard Education Press, *Harvard Educational Review, Harvard Education Letter*, Voices in Education blog, and a bi-monthly e-newsletter.

The National Association of State Boards of Education: www.nasbe.org
NASBE offers a number e-newsletters including the *Federal Update,* the *Headline Review,* and the *State Board Newsletter.*

PDK International's *Phi Delta Kappan*: www.pdkintl.org/kappan/kappan .htm
Monthly journal covering education policy and practice since 1915.

Public Education Network: http://www.publiceducation.org/newsblast _current.asp
A national association of local education funds (LEFs) and individuals working to advance public school reform in low-income commu-

nities, PEN offers a free e-mail or RSS subscription to *Newsblast*, its weekly education news resource publication.

Stateline.org: www.stateline.org/live/issues/Education
Covers state policy and politics and offers a free subscription to daily education news through an RSS Feed.

U.S. Department of Education: www.ed.gov/news/newsletters/index.html
Offers a number of free newsletters covering teaching resources, ED grant opportunities, ED activities, promising innovations, research and statistics, and violence and drug-use prevention in schools, among other subjects.

- ERIC (Education Resources Information Center) database: www .eric.ed.gov

- Free access to more than 1.2 million bibliographic records of journal articles and other education-related materials.

Notes

Introduction

1. George Emery Littlefield, *Early Schools and School-Books of New England* (Boston, MA: The Club of Odd Volumes, 1904) 82–85.
2. Deborah Land, "Local School Boards Under Review: Their Role and Effectiveness in Relation to Students' Academic Achievement," *Review of Educational Research* 72, no. 2 (2002): 235.
3. For one of the most recent attacks on local control of U.S. schools see Matt Miller, "First, Kill All the School Boards," *Atlantic Monthly*, January/February 2008. Land, however, concludes that there is more evidence that lack of funding and the complexity of state mandates have posed bigger barriers to reform than board resistance. See Land, "Local School Boards Under Review," 235.
4. Land, "Local School Boards Under Review."

Chapter One

1. Deborah Land, "Local School Boards Under Review: Their Role and Effectiveness in Relation to Students' Academic Achievement," *Review of Educational Research* 72, no. 2 (2002): 249.
2. Iowa Association of School Boards, "The Lighthouse Inquiry: School Board/Superintendent Team Behaviors in School Districts with Extreme Differences in Student Achievement" (paper presented at the American Educational Research Association annual meeting, Seattle, WA, April 2001), 7–14.
3. Richard H. Goodman, Luann Fulbright, and William G. Zimmerman Jr., *Getting There from Here: School Board Collaboration: Creating a School Governance Team Capable of Raising Student Achievement* (Arlington, VA: Educational Research Service, 1997), 3–16.
4. The Panasonic Foundation, June 16, 2009, http://www.panasonic.com/meca/foundation/default.asp.
5. The Panasonic Foundation, June 16, 2009, http://www.panasonic.com/meca/foundation/esspar.asp.
6. Patricia Mitchell, Andrew Gelber, Sophie Sa, and Scott Thompson, "Doing the Right Thing: The Panasonic Foundation's Guide for Effective School Boards" (draft, The Panasonic Foundation, Secaucus, NJ, 2009).

Chapter Two

1. Richard H. Goodman, Luann Fulbright, and William G. Zimmerman Jr., *Getting There from Here: School Board Collaboration: Creating a School Governance Team Capable of Raising Student Achievement* (Arlington, VA: Educational Research Service, 1997), 16.

2. Richard H. Goodman, "Board Duty in Retirement," *School Administrator*, December 2007.
3. Elizabeth A. City, Richard F. Elmore, Sarah E. Fiarman, and Lee Teitel, *Instructional Rounds in Education: A Network Approach to Improving Teaching and Learning* (Cambridge, MA: Harvard University Press, 2009), 2.
4. Richard F. Elmore, "The Strategic Turn in School Improvement" (unpublished chapter draft, 2008), 18.
5. City, et al., *Instructional Rounds*, 25.
6. David B. Tyack, *The One Best System: A History of American Urban Education* (Cambridge, MA: Harvard University Press, 1974), 26.
7. Katheryn W. Gemberling, Carl W. Smith, and Joseph S. Villani, *The Key Work of School Boards; A Guidebook* (Alexandria, VA: National School Boards Association, 2009), 2.
8. Now an oft-stated truism, Lighthouse Project researchers documented that boards in both high- and low-achieving districts reported satisfactory relationships with their superintendents.
9. Patricia Mitchell, Andrew Gelber, Sophie Sa, and Scott Thompson, "Doing the Right Thing: The Panasonic Foundation's Guide for Effective School Boards" (draft, Panasonic Foundation, Secaucus, NJ, 2009).

Chapter Three

1. Norfolk School District, June 19, 2009, http://www.nps.k12.va.us/index.php?option =com_content&view=article&id=596&Itemid=191.
2. Richard H. Goodman, Luann Fulbright, and William G. Zimmerman Jr., *Getting There from Here: School Board-Superintendent Collaboration: Creating a School Governance Team Capable of Raising Student Achievement* (Arlington, VA: Educational Research Service, 1997), 15.
3. Richard DuFour identified what he calls the "DRIP syndrome" in his article, "What Is a 'Professional Learning Community?'" *Educational Leadership* 61, no. 8 (2004): 10.
4. For more details on Boston's use of data, see S. Paul Reville, ed., *A Decade of Urban School Reform: Persistence and Progress in the Boston Public Schools* (Cambridge, MA: Harvard Education Press, 2007).

Chapter Four

1. Paul Donsky, "School Board's Own Grade Improving: Review Panel Sets Up Monitoring Plan," *Atlanta Journal-Constitution*, October 3, 2002.
2. Jerry Grillo, "Holding School Boards Accountable," *Georgia Trend*, June 2009.
3. Patricia Mitchell, Andrew Gelber, Sophie Sa, and Scott Thompson, "Doing the Right Thing: The Panasonic Foundation's Guide for Effective School Boards" (draft, Panasonic Foundation, Secaucus, NJ, 2009).
4. Ibid., 11.

Chapter Five

1. For a good, concise overview of arguments for and against local school boards, see John Gehring, "Essential or Obsolete? Panel Debates Value, Role of School Boards," *Education Week*, October 29, 2003, 14.

2. Frank W. Lutz and Laurence Iannaccone, "The Dissatisfaction Theory of American Democracy," in *The Future of School Board Governance: Relevancy and Revelation*, ed. Thomas L. Alsbury (Lanham, MD: Rowman & Littlefield Education, 2008), 26.

3. William J. Bushaw and Alec M. Gallup, "Americans Speak Out—Are Educators and Policy Makers Listening?: The 40th Annual Phi Delta Kappa/Gallup Poll of the Public's Attitudes Toward The Public Schools," *Phi Delta Kappan* 90, no. 1 (2008): 11–12.

4. www.nsba.org/MainMenu/ResourceCenter/SurveyStudiesandEvaluations.aspx.

Chapter Six

1. School change expert Michael Fullan estimates it takes eight years for a district to become "a good or better performing system." See Michael Fullan, *The New Meaning of Educational Change,* 3rd ed. (New York: Teachers College Press, 2001), 17.

2. Michele Erina Doyle and Mark K. Smith, "Shared Leadership," *The Encyclopedia of Informal Education*, 2001, http://www.infed.org/leadership/shared_leadership.htm.

3. National School Boards Association, *Targeting Student Learning: The School Board's Role as Policymaker* (Alexandria, VA: National School Boards Association, 2005).

4. Richard H. Goodman and William G. Zimmerman Jr. "Thinking Differently: Recommendations for 21st Century School Board/Superintendent Leadership, Governance, and Teamwork for High Student Achievement" (Marlborough, MA: New England School Development Council, and Arlington, VA: Educational Research Service, 2000).

5. Calvert County Public Schools, *Board of Education Handbook 2008: A Guide for Board Members*.

Acknowledgments

Much of the material for this book was collected during interviews and e-mail exchanges from June 2008 through July 2009. I'd like to thank the following people, in particular, for sharing their time and expertise: Barry Bishop, Kitty Blumsack, Mary Briers, Gary Brochu, Rebecca Burgett, LaChandra Butler Burks, Kamalkant Chavda, Michael Cicchetti, Christine Clair, David Cook, Mary Delagardelle, Linda Embrey, Mary Fertakis, Tommy Floyd, Andrew Gelber, Katheryn Gemberling, Tom Gentzel, Mike Gilbert, Richard Goodman, Eliza Holcomb, Gerald Kember, Kathy McFetridge, James Michel, Frank Parish, Rolf Parsons, Leni Patterson, Thomas Payzant, Dot Perkins, William Phalen, Elizabeth Reilinger, Jim Rollins, Jack Sennott, Tim Sivertson, Carl Smith, Jack Smith, Edgar Taylor, Scott Thompson, David Title, Anand Vaishnav, Joe Villani, and Doug Whitlock

I would also like to thank Harvard University professors Terrance Tivnan and Richard Elmore, who gave me invaluable advice as I embarked on the research for this book.

I would also like to acknowledge and thank Dr. Thomas Fowler-Finn, superintendent in Cambridge, Massachusetts, from 2003 to 2008. It was Tom who first opened my eyes to the power of board–superintendent collaboration to raise student achievement. His leadership made a tremendous impact on the education of six thousand or so wonderful children in every year of his service, including my own.

For answering my repeated calls for help, I want to especially thank Deborah Garson, head reference librarian at Harvard's Gutman Library; Mary Broderick, secretary-treasurer of the National School Boards Association and former chair of the NSBA's Subcommittee on Student Achievement; Mary Delagardelle, executive director of the Iowa School Boards Foundation; and Glenn Koocher and Mike Gilbert of the Massachusetts Association of School Committees.

Finally, I want to thank everyone at the Harvard Education Publishing Group for their amazing support and encouragement while I multitasked my way through this project. Special thanks, too, to editorial intern Chris Rand for help with the "Additional Resources" section.

About the Author

Nancy Walser is assistant editor of the award-winning *Harvard Education Letter*. For more than ten years, she worked as a newspaper journalist, covering education and other beats for many local, regional, and national publications, including States News Service in Washington, D.C., the *Quincy Patriot-Ledger*, the *Boston Globe*, and the *New York Times*. She also authored and published two editions of the *Parent's Guide to Cambridge Schools*.

In 1999, she was elected to the Cambridge School Committee, and served as a member of the board until 2007. During that time, she also served as secretary-treasurer and vice president of the Massachusetts Association of School Committees (MASC), attending many annual and regional conferences sponsored by the National School Boards Association and MASC.

Walser has worked at the Harvard Education Publishing Group (HEPG) since July 2006. She coauthored two recent books in the HEPG's *Spotlight* series; *Spotlight on Leadership and School Change* (Harvard Education Press, 2007) and *Spotlight on Student Engagement, Motivation, and Achievement* (Harvard Education Press, 2009). Her interview with Ronald Ferguson of the Harvard Achievement Gap Initiative and her story, "R Is for Resilience," were both finalists for Distinguished Achievement Awards in 2008 from the Association of Educational Publishers.

Walser holds a BA in English from the University of Texas at Austin, and is currently a master's candidate in the Education Policy and Management Program at the Harvard Graduate School of Education. She and her husband, Robert Buderi, live in Cambridge, Massachusetts, where their two children attend the Cambridge Rindge and Latin School.

Index